Responsible Decision Making

THE LEARNED SOCIETY OF PRAXIOLOGY

PRAXIOLOGY:
The International Annual of Practical Philosophy and Methodology Vol. 16

Responsible Decision Making

Praxiology:
The International Annual of
Practical Philosophy and
Methodology, Vol. 16

Laszlo Zsolnai

Transaction Publishers
New Brunswick (U.S.A.) and London (U.K.)

This book is printed on acid-free paper that meets the American National Standard for Permanence of Paper for Printed Library Materials.

Library of Congress Catalog Number: 20080264
ISBN: 978-1-4128-0818-7
Printed in the United States of America

Library of Congress Cataloging-in-Publication

Zsolnai, László.

Responsible decision making : praxiology : the international annual of practical philosophy and methodology, vol. 16. / László Zsolnai.

p. cm.

Includes bibliographical references and index.

ISBN 978-1-4128-0818-7 (alk. paper)

1. Decision making. 2. Choice (Psychology) 3. Ethics. 4. Praxeology. I. Title.

BF448.Z76 2008
153.8'3--dc22

20080264

Contents

Editorial

Wojciech W. Gasparski
Editor-in-Chief

"What should I do?" "How should I deal with this?" "How should I behave?" "How should I act?" we ask ourselves hundreds, if not thousands of times every day. But, this is only the first part of the sentence, while the full sentence is "What should I do...to achieve such and such?" for example to complete an assigned task, to do well before my boss or a client, to be pleased with myself, to carry out my more or less ambitious plans, to make money on the stock market, to pass an exam, to write an application, to please myself/him/her, etc. These and similar questions that we reply to all the time, consciously or not, openly or not, are decisions. The ones we see, like the tip of the iceberg, are the sharp "yes" or "no" that settles the matter one way or the other, like the president's signature or veto on a new law. The structure we do not see are the molecular and atomic decisions that we most often do not even realize we make. Here is what one Japanese decision theoretician has to say about this:

> Imagine someone deep in conversation during a meal. Eating is usually a situation of choices, as you can have more than one kind of food on your plate: meat, carrots, potatoes, etc., ready to be eaten at once. The eater may notice, having finished discussing a certain issue, that she has eaten something from his plate, i.e. she has been making choices, so her externalized behavior has successfully carried out the motoric actions necessary to eat whatever was chosen, without any conscious decision-making effort. Note that in this example, it would be wrong to say that the choices were effortless decisions made out

> of habit, because the eater can certainly engage in intentional decision-making processes. For example, she may notice a favorite tidbit on the plate and ask herself: 'Shall I eat this first, or save it for later to extend the pleasure of looking at it?'. She may give up eating the carrots because she thinks she is allergic to them etc., as long as she was paying sufficient attention to the food. But, she was not, since the conversation was so exciting that she even ate up the carrots. Choices are not decisions made out of habit (Toda 1983: pp. 257-258).

Meanwhile, eating is a relatively simple action. But, is eating a formal lunch as simple as having a quick lunch on the go? Probably not, given the well-known American saying that "there's no such thing as a free lunch." A formal meal can be a test of who we are, an opportunity to arrange some important matter etc. Circumstances lend a new dimension to our ordinary decisions. As our actions become more complicated, our decisions—the foundation of subsequent success or the quicksand of failure—become increasingly difficult, increasingly complex. It was not without reason that French praxiologist Arnold Kaufmann, author of *The Science of Decision-making: An Introduction to Praxiology* (1968), spoke of a kind of bio-praxiology—the instinctive capacity for efficient behavior related to strategies of defense, existence and change, manifested by living organisms, namely animals and plants. This capacity is exhibited in standard situations catalogued in reaction patterns inherited from previous generations and those learned at the start of the individual's life, like the way in which an adult bird forces its progeny to fly by pecking the chicks out of the nest.

We as people also inherit a small store of skills, and acquire other skills—called *praxias*—when we learn to catch a dummy or rattle as we lie in our cradle, and then as we change from a baby crawling on all fours into a proudly erect lord of all beings. Over a century and a dozen years ago, Alfred Victor Espinas, the founder of praxiology, wrote that human skills, like animal instincts, have two important features—heredity and adaptation. Moreover, skills are the effect of reflection which assumes invention, initiative and freedom. Useful skills are called *techniques* (from the Greek *techne*), and knowledge about them is *technologie generale,* or praxiology (Alexandre & Gasparski 2000).

Praxiology is like the prose of Monsieur Jourdain, the protagonist of Moliere's *The Bourgeois Gentleman:* everybody uses it but only some know *what* they are thinking, *what* they are saying, *what* they are doing. Most of them (us) remain "bourgeois" all their lives (regardless of whether they live in a hut or a palace) without knowing that they are behaving (we are behaving) praxiologically, even if they become "gentlemen" (quote or unquote). Only some, who are lucky enough to meet the Philosopher like Moliere's character did, will become gentlemen of action *par excellence,* able to distinguish prose from poetry.

Everybody—whether they be a "bourgeois" or a gentleman (in quotes or not)—acts while submerged in the "bubble" of their practical situation defined by the values they profess and believe in, and the facts they perceive as a consequence. "I" is the most important, as expressed in the way the English language capitalizes it. "YOU," whether singular or plural, is written in small letters, just "you." For "I," "YOU" are "you," for "YOU"—"you" are "I," and "I" am "you." Even if one advises "I" to love "YOU", it is to love "YOU" "as thyself." Man is perhaps the measure of all things, but not of love, the measure of love is "I." This leads to a morality in which "I" should not do to "YOU" what "I" finds unpleasant ("do unto others as you would have them do unto you"). Coming into contact with the "bubbles" of the practical situations of others, "I" is surprised to find a displeased "YOU." Meanwhile, why should "YOU" find pleasant what "I" find pleasant?

Bio-praxiological efficiency in decision-making is not enough, *praxias* can be helpful but also insufficient. One needs to reach for Espinas's skills—*techniques*—of the social group to which "I" and some of "YOU" belong. "I" and all the closer "YOU"—these are "WE," the more distant "YOU"—are "THEY." "WE" are "WE" because we are similar to one another physically and axiologically as well as praxiologically. "THEY" are different. Protecting similarity, we create "OUR" morality, which makes "THEM" accuse us of relativism. "WE" defend ourselves by saying that "THEY" profess relativism by not recognizing "OUR" morality, because it is "WE" who are right. We strengthen our arguments with our politics and our law. To be able to exist, we have to run the economy. Matters start getting complicated, some decisions influence others, some people influence other people. Sometimes to good effect, sometimes not. It all depends on responsibility, on how it is understood, and on readiness to assume responsibility. The intersection of the two disciplines—praxiology and theory of decision—could be helpful.

To review contributions to praxiology and studies on decision-making, one may refer to the following works: Oskar Lange (Gasparski 1992), Arnold Kaufmann (1968, 2000), Herbert A. Simon (1992), Jozef Kozielecki (1981), George J. Klir (1992), Ladislav Tondl (1992), Tadeusz Tyszka (1998), to mention just a few well-known authors.

I am not going to summarize their articles and books, leaving the task to those who would like to learn more about the interrelations between the two disciplines. Let me recount the following instead. It was at the Fifth Research Conference on Subjective Probability, Utility, and Decision Making (SPUDM) organized in Darmstadt in 1975 that Professor Klemens Szaniawski, the leading decision theoretician both in Poland and elsewhere, and I presented a paper on "Praxiology and Decision Theory". The contribution was included in the Section of the *Proceedings* (Jungermann & Zeeuw 1997) that was devoted to the perspectives for further inquiry in decision theory.

The present book by Laszlo Zsolnai, a volume in the *Praxiology* series, proves that the decision made by Helmut Jungermann and Gerard de Zeeuw, editors of the proceedings, was right. It is *the* perspective.

Szaniawski and I noticed that both praxiology and decision theory study phenomena of the same kind. Moreover, their points of view are very similar, sometimes identical for they "try to evaluate human goal directed actions in terms of such criteria as efficacy, i.e., effectiveness with respect to the goal, efficiency of means applied, and the like." (Gasparski & Szaniawski 1977: p. 491). We expressed the hope that although they differed in outlook the differences may turn out to be a blessing in the sense that they would act as a stimulus to reappraisal of what is usually taken for granted *(ibid,* 492). The following was suggested:

> [...] decision theory deals with closed, well defined sets of choice, whereas praxiology analyzes the adaptation of behavior to a goal, no limitation of the agent's inventiveness having been presupposed. Also, it goes to show that some specifically decision theoretic concepts can be profitably used in praxiological analysis.
>
> Does it work the other way round? What profit, if any, can be expected from an attempt to adapt praxiological concepts to the needs of decision theory? This is largely a matter of conjecture. It seems, however, that in the present stage of decision theory's development it may prove quite fruitful to look at the same problems from some other, e.g., praxiological point of view.
>
> It has frequently been pointed out that classical paradigm of decision theory (strategy, states of the world, utilities) has been exploited to such a degree that it has almost outlived its usefulness. Some radical change of the paradigm is generally felt to be necessary. It is not clear, however, what kind of model would ensure a deeper insight into the process of rational decision making. The praxiological approach may turn out to be helpful here, precisely because of the basic difference in the way of looking at things; the stress is laid on the goal, rather than on the closed set of available acts. (Gasparski & Szaniawski 1997: p. 502).

The proposal written by Laszlo Zsolnai is an attempt to build such a model of making decisions both effective and efficient as well as accepted from an ethical point of view. Therefore the model is much broader than purely analytical (White 1975). It says how to act rather than limit one's reflection to decision analysis of actions already performed, trying to combine decision and praxiological analysis (Gasparski 2000) of human conduct. The proposed model enlarges the scope of the debate and suggests new avenues of both rational and responsible decision making.

Navigare necesse est, vivere non est necesse, it is necessary to sail, it is not necessary to live, says Plutarch in the words familiar to those who, aware of having to struggle against waves, winds and storms, know the value of the ability to reach their destination, sometimes a very distant one. People, contrary to birds migrating to warmer climates for winter and returning in the spring, have to learn the art of navigation. Since they have to—in the sense that it is essential to enable them to avoid practical mistakes, then they can. What skills, then, must we master as human beings, especially when we need to make not only elementary decisions but also decisions that affect the existence, health and even lives of others? First and foremost, we should acquire the skill of acquiring skills, i.e. the skill of acquiring knowledge. Only then will we stand a chance of reacting to things that are improbable today but could become a fact tomorrow. Also essential is the skill of designing, i.e. preparing actions conceptually in order to make decisions before irreversible changes occur. Finally, it is essential to master the skill of multidimensional judgment within the space defined by the "triple E" of effectiveness, efficiency and ethicality.

References

Gasparski, Wojciech, Szaniawski, Klemens, 1997, Praxiology and Decision Theory, in: Jungermann, Helmut, and De Zeuuwe, Gerard (eds.), 1997, *Decision Making and Change in Human Affairs,* Reidel, Dordrecht, pp. 491-506.

Gasparski, Wojciech, 1992, Oskar Lange's Considerations on Interrelations between Praxiology, Cybernetics, and Economics, in: Auspitz, J. Lee, Gasparski, Wojciech, W., Mlicki, Marek, K., Szaniawski, Klemens (eds.), *Praxiologies and the Philosophy of Economics,* Transaction Publishers, New Brunswick (U.S.A.)-London (U.K.), pp. 449^66.

Gasparski, Wojciech, W., 2000, Ergonomics and Praxiology, *Theoretical Issues in Ergonomics Science,* Vol. 1, No. 4, pp. 366-377.

Jungermann, Helmut, and De Zeuuwe, Gerard (eds.), 1997, *Decision Making and Change in Human Affairs,* Reidel, Dordrecht.

Kaufmann, Arnold, 1968, *The Science of Decision-making: An Introduction to Praxeology,* World University Library, Weidenfeld and Nicolson, London.

Kaufmann, Arnold, 2000, The Science of Decision-making, in: Alexandra, Victor in cooperation with Gasparski, Wojciech W., *The Roots of Praxiology: French Action Theory from Bourdeau and Espinas to Present Days,* Transaction Publishers, New Brunswick (U.S.A.)-London (U.K.), pp. 183-198.

Klir, George, J., 1992, The Role of Methodological Principles of Uncertainty in Economics, in: Auspitz, J. Lee, Gasparski, Wojciech, W., Mlicki, Marek, K., Szaniawski, Klemens (eds.), *Praxiologies and the Philosophy of Economics,* Transaction Publishers, New Brunswick (U.S.A.)-London (U.K.), pp. 61-92.

Kozielecki, Jozef, 1981, *Psychological Decision Theory.* Reidel, Dordrecht.

Simon, Herbert, A., 1992, Methodological Foundations of Economics, in: Auspitz, J. Lee, Gasparski, Wojciech, W., Mlicki, Marek, K., Szaniawski, Klemens (eds.), *Praxiologies and the Philosophy of Economics,* Transaction Publishers, New Brunswick (U.S.A.)-London (U.K.), pp. 25-42.

Szaniawski, Klemens, 1992, Probability in Social Decision, in: Auspitz, J. Lee, Gasparski, Wojciech, W., Mlicki, Marek, K., Szaniawski, Klemens (eds.), *Praxiologies and the Philosophy of Economics,* Transaction Publishers, New Brunswick (U.S.A.)-London (U.K.), pp. 599-604.

Toda, M., 1983, What Happens at the Moment of Decision? Meta-decisions, Emotions, and Volitions, in: L. Sjoberg, T. Tyszka, J.A. Wise (eds.), *Human Decision-making,* Doxa, Bodafors.

Tondl, L., 1992, System Evaluation of Rational Actions, in: Auspitz, J. Lee, Gasparski, Wojciech, W., Mlicki, Marek, K., Szaniawski, Klemens (eds.), *Praxiologies and the Philosophy of Economics,* Transaction Publishers, New Brunswick (U.S.A.)-London (U.K.), pp. 635-654.

Tyszka, Tadeusz, 1998, Two Pairs of Conflicting Motives in Decision Making, *Organizational Behavior and Human Decision Making,* No. 74, pp. 1-23.

White, Douglas, J., 1975, *Decision Methodology,* Wiley, London.

Foreword

Ethical decision making, as an object of close examination, has long been of considerable concern though to a relatively few individuals and professions. However, in recent years, the examination of this important issue has greatly expanded. Extended discussions of ethical decision making can be found in articles and books by ethicists, psychologists, sociologists, economists, as well as academics in marketing and management, to name only some of the disciplines that have taken up this subject. These investigations come at the confluence of a wide variety of influences: interest in applied and practical ethics (e.g., in business, medicine, and the military) has greatly grown in the last thirty years. Developments in technology promise greater safety for customers but do not answer ethical questions regarding how much safety is required and who should determine this. There is today widespread acknowledgment of corruption in countries around the world and the importance of reducing or eliminating it. Globalization has brought increased attention to the policies of multinationals and international organizations that can affect the quality of the environment on an international scale.

Some of this interest in ethical decision is descriptive and explanatory in nature. What forces and influences encourage or foster the ethical decisions which people make? These discussions do not speak to whether actual cases of ethical decision making are correct or incorrect, but rather, for example, to the circumstances that brought them about, how they differ (or do not differ) between genders and cultures, or the influence of corporate culture, peer pressure, and schemas or scripts on people when they make ethical decisions.

Other discussions of ethical decision making take a normative approach. Here the aim is to arrive at various principles, rules, models, or processes whereby people faced with practical moral problems might resolve them in ways that are arguably justified. At their best, these discussions are not moralistic. They do not turn all of our experiences into simple, or even simplistic, formulas. Rather they seek to bring to bear the latest knowledge and experience humans have regarding how ethical decision making would best be undertaken so as to resolve moral problems. Here ethicists examine the role of principles, rules, game theory, theories of negotiation, etc. in an attempt to provide guidance for ethical decision making.

It is just this that Professor Zsolnai, Professor and Director of the Budapest Ethics Center at the Corvinus University of Budapest, undertakes in the present book that contributes to this important discussion. The basic theme of his book is the development of a normative (not a descriptive) model of responsible choice. That is, he wishes to present to the reader a way of resolving moral dilemmas that is superior to other previous accounts of ethical decision making. To do this he develops a normative responsible choice model that is applicable to real persons, not ideal ones. This means looking at complex choice situations, not simple or ideal ones. His model is intended both for individual persons and organizations both of which he considers to be moral agents. And, to drive his arguments home, he applies his account to several case studies in the course of this book, e.g. cases involving Donna (a case derived from Amartya Sen), the Ford Pinto, the World Bank (its environmental policy). He does not rest, however, simply with an account of ethical decision in specific instances, but in his last chapter applies his views, albeit briefly, to the idea of the responsible person. In this chapter he describes a balanced path between the under-socialized and the over-socialized person, one who is "securely autonomous".

Importantly, Professor Zsolnai develops this model not simply in a priori manner, as some have sought to do, but rather by drawing on a broad range of knowledge regarding ethical decision making from contemporary ethics, sociological and psychological theories of human choice, decision theory and economics. This is a worthy undertaking, regarding which Professor Zsolnai challenges us to participate.

In the process of developing his model he criticizes the universal substitutability of values, market fundamentalist views, and various economic models of choice. These are important current issues that Professor Zsolnai addresses. The upshot of his argument is a notion of responsible choice as the synthesis of a reverence for ethical norms, rational goal achievement, and respect for others. He argues that this synthesis occurs through "the selection of the least worse alternative in the decision space of deontological, goal achievement and stakeholder values." Hence, underlying Professor Zsolnai's approach is an appeal to maximin rules that permit only limited trade offs. His argument for this view is based upon his review of the work of a wide variety of outstanding scholars, including Sen, Elster, Jonas, Mansbridge, Goodpaster, Simon, Tversky, Kahneman, Etzioni, and Frankfurt.

Professor Zsolnai's discussion of this important topic is a welcome contribution, especially inasmuch as it brings to bear the contribution of a wide range of authors from North America and Europe in his effort to develop an integrated theory of ethical decision making. Particularly desirable is Professor Zsolnai's application of this model to practical cases, as well as its extension towards an account of the responsible person. At times Professor Zsolnai provides us with broad surveys of these views and extended game theoretical analyses of ethical decision making. At other times he proceeds through succinct statements of the views of the authors on whom he draws in order to build his own model of responsible choice. At one point Professor Zsolnai comments that "responsibility is not a luxury; rather it is a precondition of life worthy to live". Professor Zsolnai challenges us to face this important topic through the thoughtful answers he has provided.

George G. Brenkert
Director
Georgetown Business Ethics Institute
Georgetown University, Washington D.C.

Preface

When I was studying economics in the 1980s, I developed an aversion to the rational choice theory. I was a devoted friend of rationality, but I felt that rationality is about other things than how to maximize one's utility function. As a junior researcher at the Department of Sociology of the Budapest University of Economic Sciences, I realized that maximizing the utility function is a rather degenerate form of what Max Weber called goal rationality ("*zveckrationalitat*").

The ethical implications of the Homo Oeconomicus model seemed to me horrifying, especially from the ecological point of view that I had gradually adopted in the mid-1980s. During that time I had read Hans Jonas' book *The Imperative of Responsibility* and concluded that responsibility has possibly nothing to do with the rational choice theory.

In 1988 Herbert A. Simon came to Budapest for the Fourth International Conference on Foundations and Applications of Utility, Risk and Decision Theory. I had the privilege of organizing Professor Simon's program in Budapest and presented a paper for the conference under the title "Morally Rational Decisions" (Zsolnai, L. 1991). In my paper I developed a framework in which rationality, understood as process proposed by Herbert Simon, functions within a higher-level context of moral considerations.

In 1990-91 I was a visiting scholar at the University of California at Berkeley. I had the opportunity to work with Edwin M. Epstein in the field of business ethics, and I learned at that time about the tremendous criticism the rational choice theory was undergoing in the USA and elsewhere, which continues into the present.

I remember quite well my discussion with Epstein about Jane Mansbridge's excellent book *Beyond Self-Interest* (Mansbridge, J. [ed.]: 1990). I accepted the point made by Mansbridge that duty, self-interest, and love possibly represent the three irreducible motives of human behavior.

Professor Epstein involved me in organizing the Second International Conference on Public Service Ethics held in Sienna in 1992. I was invited to give a lecture on rationality and morality. In my paper I proposed a model of decision making in which deontological considerations come first, giving subsequent but equal attention to the goal-achievement of the decision maker and the effects of the decision on the other parties, the stakeholders (Zsolnai, L. 1992).

I later received comments on my paper from Kenneth E. Goodpaster, from the University of Saint Thomas in Minnesota. He wrote that my model was nice but required good hard work to elaborate. The good hard work followed in Budapest. For the years 1993 through 1995, I received a research grant from the Hungarian National Science Foundation (OTKA) to elaborate my model of ethical decision making. I have relinquished the position that deontological considerations have any supremacy over consequentialist ones. I was searching for a model of the balancing approach in which the decision maker equalizes values across different dimensions.

I asked Professor Jozsef Kindler, a specialist in decision theory, and his son-in-law, Morton Gyombolai, a mathematician, for suggestions. They proposed that I should try the "maximin" rule. The maximin rule proposes choosing the least worst alternative in the value space of the choice. I realized that it does work. I wrote my summarizing paper at the end of my research project under the title "Moral Responsibility and Economic Choice" (Zsolnai, L. 1997). The basic structure of the ethical-decision-making model was ready.

For the Academic Year 1996 through 1997, I received an invitation from the Netherlands Institute for Advanced Study in the Humanities and Social Sciences (NIAS) to spend a semester in Wassenaar, the Netherlands. It was an inspiring place for me to write the first draft of my book on ethical decision making. From 1998 through 1999 I was absorbed in other projects in Budapest. However, I did produce the Hungarian version of my book, which was published in September 2000.

In 2000 I was a Connelly Visiting Scholar in Business Ethics at Georgetown University in Washington, D.C. The hospitality and support provided by Professor George Brenkert made it possible for me to complete a new version of my book.

The manuscript was left untouched for several years, until I received an inquiry from Professor Wojciech Gasparski, the editor-in-chief of the Praxiology Series of Transaction Publishers. I was glad to respond to his kind interest and prepared the final version of the manuscript between 2005 and 2006.

At the end of my book I arrived at the idea of the responsible person, which is what I have always aspired to become. Let me hope that I am not alone in holding such a high moral aspiration.

Budapest, October 2006

Laszlo Zsolnai

Acknowledgements

I am very grateful to my masters in different disciplines, although none of them ever served as an official university tutor for me. I learned economics from Janos Kornai, Tibor Liska and Andras Brody. Jozsef Kindler introduced me to decision theory and evaluation research. Pal Juhasz-Nagy acquainted me with ecology and mathematical modeling. Last but not least my father, Jozsef Zsolnai, introduced me to philosophy and scientific research methodology. The intellectual impacts of all of these excellent minds have been significant in shaping the research project that resulted in this book.

I received comments and suggestions on different points of my conception of ethical decision making from the late Herbert A. Simon (Carnegie Melon University), Edwin M. Epstein (University of California at Berkeley), Kenneth E. Goodpaster (St. Thomas University, Minnesota), Stefano Zamagni (University of Bologna), Marinus Van Ijzendoorn (Leiden University), Hans Radder (Free University of Amsterdam), Gerald Postema (University of North Carolina at Chapel Hill), Gian-Vittorio Caprara (University of Rome, "La Sapienza"), Peter Pruzan (Copenhagen Business School), and George Brenkert (Georgetown University). Naturally, the full responsibility for the responsible decision making model elaborated in the book is exclusively mine.

The research grant from the Hungarian National Science Foundation (OTKA) for 1993 through 1995 and the financial support and hospitality of the Netherlands Institute for Advanced Study in the Humanities and Social Sciences (NIAS) from 1996 through 1997 are greatly appreciated. The John F. Connelly Program in Business Ethics financed my stay at Georgetown University in March and April 2000, when I finished the earlier version of the book.

The Corvinus University of Budapest and its former rector, Attila Chikan, and former dean, Sandor Kerekes, provided me with a supportive environment for the struggle with the difficult problems of ethics and economics. Finally, my deep appreciation and love go to my wife, Julianna Farkas, who not only tolerates my enthusiasm but seems to even enjoy it.

Laszlo Zsolnai

Notes on Terminology

The book deals with issues common to *economics, ethics,* and *decision theory.* For this reason terms are used from all of these disciplines. This may occasionally create difficulties because these disciplines often use different terms to represent the same things. The usage of the terms is careful throughout the book; however, some note on the terminology might be helpful for the reader.

The terms "decision alternative" and "course of action" are used interchangeably. Similarly, the terms "decision maker" and "agent," and "decision" and "choice" refer pair wisely to the same entities. Finally, "value" and "payoff are generally synonymous.

The terms "stakeholders" and "affected parties" refer interchangeably to beings affected by the choice of the decision maker. The terms "rationality" and "responsibility," however, each have several meanings. The relevant meanings of these crucial terms are always indicated in the given context.

I use the term "deontology" in a rather broad sense referring to norm-regarding evaluation. So in this book, deontology refers to no form of deontological ethics.

Mathematical notations have been reduced to a minimum, but in some chapters the mathematical representation of the argumentation is necessary.

List of Figures

List of Tables

1. Introduction: Responsibility and Choice

The main idea of the book is that responsibility implies choice. This means that the responsibility perceived by the decision maker largely determines his or her choice. The greater the adequacy of the decision maker's conception of responsibility in the given situation, the greater the chance that she or he will make a decision which is an appropriate response to the situation.

In the praxiological tradition, Wojciech Gasparski introduces the "triple E" criteria for judging human actions. The triple E refers to effectiveness, efficiency, and ethics (Gasparski, W. 2002).

Jozef Maria Bochenski, a Polish philosopher affiliated with the University of Freiburg, introduced the differentiation between thinking and serious thinking. The objective of the latter form of thinking is knowledge, a cognitive value. Gasparski argues that a similar concept should be introduced to differentiate between action per se and action that is aimed at economic value. Thus, economic action would constitute serious action. Seriousness is measured by positive values of the effectiveness dimensions of the action. But seriousness also requires that the social-axiological context of actions be taken into consideration, under pain of any of them being considered unacceptable in a given culture.

The analysis of human actions in terms of the triple E is the condition for the highest-ranking of serious actions—wisdom. Wisdom is the technique that refers to the strong character of the acting subject. Praxiology, says Bochenski, is one of those disciplines in which we can find assertions corresponding to the injunctions of wisdom (Gasparski, W. 2002).

In my view effectiveness, efficiency and ethics reflect three irreducible aspects of human choices. Stakeholders, goals, and ethical norms constitute the value-space within which decisions are made. Responsible decision making means finding an optimal balance among the differing "callings" in human choice situations.

The aim of this book is to develop a normative model of responsible decision making that is consistent with the main psychological and sociological theories of human choice behavior.

Decision scientist Kenneth R. MacCrimmon made important distinctions among different types of decision theories. Decision theory deals with either *"is"* or *"ought."* The former means that the theory focuses on how people do make decisions while the latter means that theory focuses on how people should make decisions. Both "is" and "ought" theories can assume either real persons or ideal persons (MacCrimmon, K.R. 1995: pp. 256-267).

In this way we can arrive at a total of four clusters: (i) "Is" theories assuming real persons; (ii) "Ought" theories assuming real persons; (iii) "Is" theories assuming ideal persons; (iv) "Ought" theories assuming ideal persons.

Table 1 shows the different types of decision theory.

TABLE 1
Differing Types of Decision Theory

	Assuming real persons	**Assuming ideal persons**
Focusing on "is"	How real persons do make decisions?	How ideal persons do make decisions?
Focusing on "ought"	How ideal persons should make decisions?	How ideal persons should make decisions?

Source: Adapted from MacCrimmon, K.R. 1995.

The responsible decision making model developed in this book deals with the category of "ought" but assumes real persons, not ideal ones. Although real people may not make decisions as they ought to according to the responsible choice model advanced here, they are capable of using the model directly in real world situations if they want.

The most important choices are made in complex choice situations. In such situations the choice has wide-ranging consequences, and not only the decision maker but also other parties are affected by the outcome of the choice.

Responsibility is unavoidably present in complex choice situations. This is the main reason the standard economic model of choice is not adequate in solving large, multi-agent problems of economics and public policy.

In the literature, the term "responsibility" is used in different ways in a variety of contexts. The book focuses on prospective moral responsibility in the decision-making context. I do not differentiate between persons and organizations. The responsible-decision-making model can be applied to both types of moral agents.

A lot of work has been done in ethics on the topic of retrospective moral responsibility. However, we have only one comprehensible theory of prospective moral responsibility. It is presented by Hans Jonas in his opus magnum *The Imperative of Responsibility* (Jonas, H. 1979, 1984).

According to Jonas, responsibility means caring for the beings involved in our actions. This imperative presents a basic nonreciprocal duty toward other beings, including nonhuman beings and future human beings.

Jonas' theory of responsibility has important similarities with Carol Gilligan's understanding of female morality. Gilligan interprets the moral experience of women as an ethic of care, which is contrasted with the ethic of rights represented by men. In mature morality these two disparate modes of moral experience are connected. A mature concept of responsibility should integrate the reverence for rights emphasized by men and the nonviolence of care represented by women.

The standard model of choice in economics and other social sciences is the well-known rational choice model. The model states that the agent should maximize her or his utility function in order to be considered rational. It requires that the agent's preferences are transitive and complete. (In circumstances of risk and uncertainty there are additional requirements, such as continuity and independence concerning the agent's preferences.)

The rational choice model represents a formal theory that says nothing about what human agents prefer or should prefer. Regardless of whether their preferences are self-interested, altruistic or even sadomasochistic, the agents may be equally rational in making their own choices. I refer to this model of choice as the weak form of rationality.

In economics and other social science literature, we often find a much stronger version of rationality. Assumptions of self-interest and perfect knowledge are added to the rational choice model. This is the famous Homo Oeconomicus model, according to which agents maximize their self-interest under perfect knowledge of the consequences. This model has a substantive claim about what people want or should want. I refer to the Homo Oeconomicus model as the strong form of rationality.

Both the weak and the strong forms of rationality have been heavily criticized by psychologists, sociologists, economists, political scientists, and philosophers on descriptive as well as on normative grounds.

Nobel laureate economist Herbert A. Simon states that the rational choice model has very strong claims concerning the cognitive capacity of human beings. Real world people have rather poor cognitive capacity and the information available to them is quite limited in most cases. Real world agents are not capable of maximizing their utility functions (if they have any). Instead of maximizing, they make "satisficing" decisions. According to Simon, human rationality is essentially bounded.

Princeton University psychologist Daniel Kahneman criticizes the rational choice model on the basis of experimental research. It has been found that people usually make myopic choices. They lack the skill to predict the utility of their chosen options. In addition, people have fallible memories that lead to incorrect evaluations of their past experiences.

Behavioral-decision researchers have discovered that people systematically violate the axioms of rationality, especially in circumstances involving risk and uncertainty. The most famous cases are the Allots' paradox, the Ellsberg's problem, the preference-reversal effect, and the framing effect. These violations of rationality are so fundamental that no hybrid, nearly rational model can possibly capture this type of behavior.

Nobel laureate economist Amartya Sen criticizes both forms of rationality. He refers to the weak form as internal consistency of choice and to the strong form as maximization of self-interest. Sen shows that internal consistency cannot guarantee a person's rationality. A person can always choose exactly the opposite of what would enhance those things she or he wants or values. Some correspondence between the choice and the aims and values of the agent is certainly required.

Sen notices that selfishness as a universal pattern of human choice behavior may be false, but universal selfishness as a requirement of rationality is patently absurd. The self-interest view of rationality does not reflect the complex motivations of agents in their economic affairs (duty, loyalty, and goodwill in addition to self-interest).

Cornell University economist Robert Frank emphasizes the strategic role of emotions in making choices. Frank shows that passions often serve our self-interest because we face important problems that are simply unsolvable by rational action. The modular-brain theory seems to support Frank's arguments. According to this new theory, the brain is organized into a host of separate modules. Not all modules are equally well connected to the central language module of the brain that is viewed as the center of our rational consciousness. The rational choice model reflects only the working of the language module of the left hemisphere of the human brain. However, a lot of information is simply not accessible to the language module of our brain.

Columbia University sociologist Jon Elster contrasts rational action with norm-guided behavior. While rational action is outcome oriented, social norms are not. Social norms have a grip on the mind that is based on the strong emotions that their violations can arouse. According to Elster, human actions are determined jointly by self-interest and social norms. Social norms are only partly shaped by self-interest. They have an independent motivating power.

Communitarian philosophers such as Charles Taylor, Michael Sandel and Alasdair MacIntyre forcefully criticize the liberal conception of the self, which is the underlying assumption of the rational choice model. They consider this conception of the self as being basically an atomistic one that denies the relational, intersubjective nature of human agency. It also neglects the constitutive role of communities and moral traditions in the deliberation of choices individuals ultimately make.

Sociologist Amitai Etzioni has developed the "I & We" paradigm, which sees individuals in perpetual dialogue with their communities. Etzioni describes human choice behavior as an attempt at finding a balance between pleasure and morality. He advances a co-determination model in which choice is affected by both pleasure and morality, which are in turn partly shaped by one another.

The rational choice model can also be criticized from an environmental point of view because the sustainability of natural systems cannot be assured on the basis of individual self-interested choices.

Feminist criticism states that the rational choice model presupposes a male-biased conception of the human person known as the separative self.

Harvard University political scientist Jane Mansbridge has developed a tripartite scheme of human motivation. She identifies duty, self-interest, and love as irreducible motives of human behavior. This model goes back to David Hume, who acknowledges the rich variety of human behavior when speaking about principle-driven, interest-driven, and affection-driven actions. Mansbridge favors the coincidence of duty and love with self-interest. She argues that in society, some "ecological niche" should be arranged for non self-interested behavior to be protected from self-interested behavior on the part of others.

Choice can best be seen as problem solving. The agent experiences some tension between the perceived state of affairs and the desired state of affairs. There is a gap between "is" and "ought" in the given situation.

Complex choice situations usually present ill-structured problems where the solution is far from clear or trivial. Russell L. Ackoff coined the term "mess" to describe such decision situations. The decision maker should use some heuristics for framing the decision he or she is facing. First the decision maker sets his or her aspirations concerning the solution of the problematic situation. However, other normative-affective factors are also at work, namely, ethical norms that apply in the given context and perceived other parties that can be affected by the outcome of the decision maker's choice.

Ethical norms represent a subclass of social norms. They pose specific demands, which place duties on the decision maker. A great variety of duties may apply in complex choice situations. The decision maker may have perfect or imperfect duties that are either universal or special.

The affected parties are often called stakeholders in the realms of business and public administration. Stakeholders are those parties that can be affected by the choice of the decision maker, and they are not limited to individuals, groups and organizations. Natural entities such as biological creatures, ecosystems and the Earth as a whole might also be included among the stakeholders of a decision. Similarly, future generations should be considered as stakeholders if their positions are affected by the choice of the decision maker.

Goals and alternatives are not prearranged and given for the decision maker. The applicable ethical norms, the aspirations of the decision maker, and the perceived stakeholders together form the normative-affective basis that serves in the search for goals and alternatives. Goals and alternatives are not independent of each other but rather co-evolve. The generated alternatives influence the goals that are already in motion.

Business ethicist Kenneth E. Goodpaster has presented the most developed model of moral responsibility in an economic context. He proposes that moral responsibility should be understood as rationality and respect in making decisions.

Rationality is described by the following attributes: (i) lack of impulsiveness, (ii) care in mapping out alternatives and consequences, (iii) clarity about goals and purposes, and (iv) attention to details of implementation. This concept of rationality resembles Max Weber's "zweckrationalitat" and is closely related to Herbert Simon's notion of procedural rationality. It does not imply that the decision maker is preoccupied with maximizing her or his self-interest only.

Respect means having a special awareness of and concern for the effects of one's decisions and policies on others. It goes beyond seeing others as being merely instrumental to accomplishing one's own purposes and goals. Respect for the lives of others involves taking their needs and interests seriously.

Goodpaster's responsibility model is largely a consequentialist model of choice. It seems to favor an evaluation of the decision alternatives in terms of consequences from the perspectives of both the decision maker and the stakeholders.

A consequentialist accounting can be criticized on different grounds. In complex choice situations there are phenomena whose consequentialist evaluation presents decision traps. We may think of marginal contributions as those described by American ecologist Garret Hardin in his famous "tragedy of the commons" model, effects that are distant and/or dispersed in space and time, and consequences that are highly uncertain and partly unforeseeable.

The consequentialist accounting is also challenged from a deontological point of view. The essence of deontology is that the value of an act is determined not by its consequences but by its conformity to a relevant moral principle or duty. Philosopher Thomas Nagel generates crucial examples in which the agent has good deontological reason not to do something unless it would lead to good consequences.

I think it is better to deconstruct the ambiguous notion of "respect." I propose to define respect by referring exclusively to altruistic orientation toward the affected parties. Also, I propose to introduce deontological considerations as a separate component into the model of responsibility.

In this way we get a robust model of moral responsibility. Responsible decision making is characterized as a synthesis of deontological considerations, rationality in goal achievement, and respect for the stakeholders. This model might be called the 3R model since responsible decision making equals reverence for the applying ethical norms plus rationality in goal achievement plus respect for the affected parties.

To arrive at a realistic and operationalized model of ethical decision making some basic findings of decision psychology should be thoroughly investigated.

The prospect theory developed by Daniel Kahneman and Amos Tversky is an alternative theory of decision making under conditions of risk. Based on their experimental studies, Kahneman and Tversky conclude that the value function of decision makers is convex for gains and concave for losses. They also state that decision makers are more sensitive to losses than to gains.

The matching law was formulated by Harvard psychologist Richard J. Herrnstein after decades of experimental study. It states that individuals tend to equalize reinforcement across alternatives. The salient difference between the matching law and the utility maximization principle is that matching is based on average returns instead of marginal returns. The matching law predicts that individuals allocate suboptimally because they equalize average satisfaction at some expense in overall gains.

Complex choice situations often present incommensurability for the decision maker because of differing value dimensions. It is observed empirically that decision makers seek to avoid making tradeoffs across incommensurable value dimensions. This regularity has been confirmed by the game experimental results of the Nobel laureate German economist Reinhard Selten.

The natural heuristic of decision makers facing incommensurability is depicted by Herbert A. Simon. He states that decision makers concentrate initially on improving the most critical problem area until it has achieved a satisfactory level of performance.

Complex choice situations have the following basic features: (i) more than one decision alternative is available to the decision maker; (ii) at least one ethical norm applies to the decision maker; (iii) the decision maker has at least one goal to achieve; (iv) at least one stakeholder is present in the situation.

Responsible decision making involves finding and implementing the decision alternative that best fits to the idea of responsibility in the given context of choice.

Kahneman-Tversky type of value functions can be introduced to determine the deontological, goal achievement, and stakeholder values of the decision alternatives. In this way every decision alternative is evaluated from three different perspectives, namely the perspective of the ethical norms, the perspective of the decision maker's goals, and the perspective of the stakeholders.

I propose using the maximin rule for making responsible choices. It implies the maximization of the minimum payoff of decision alternatives. The rule is intuitively well known to chess players who select the branch that will provide the best response in the face of an aggressive opponent. However, it was formally described as early as 1912 by the Austrian logician Ernest Zermello. The rule was developed further in game theory by the Hungarian-American mathematical genius John von Neumann.

Responsible decision making means selecting of the least worst alternative in the decision space of deontological, goal-achievement, and stakeholder values. The underlying principle is that the decision maker should find an optimal balance across different value dimensions.

Responsible choice provides a Pareto optimal result in the sense that given the set of decision alternatives, it is not possible to increase the payoff in any decision alternative in one value dimension without decreasing its payoff in at least one other value dimension.

Rational choice can be considered a reduced form of responsible decision making. If there are neither applying ethical norms nor affected parties in the choice situation, then the ethical-decision-making model falls into the rational choice model.

The procedural model of responsible decision making can be summarized as follows:

(I) Framing the choice situation by
- (i) identifying the applying ethical norms;
- (ii) mapping out the affected parties;
- (iii) defining goals and generating alternatives.

(II) Multiple evaluation of each alternative regarding
  (i) the ethical norms;
  (ii) the goals to be achieved;
  (iii) the affected parties.
(III) Selecting the alternative whose minimum payoff is maximal in the decision space of deontological, goal-achievement, and stakeholder values.

Complex real world cases can be solved by using the responsible-choice framework. Multiple satisficing solutions are attainable if equal attention is paid to all of the relevant value dimensions, that is, if deontological, goal achievement and stakeholder considerations are regarded simultaneously and the least worst options are consistently chosen.

The responsible-decision-making model can provide new insights into some basic problems of economics and public policy.

John Rawls' famous principle of justice can be defended on the basis of responsible choices made by people when they know perfectly well their own positions in a society. Responsible people in average, above-average and below-average positions will accept the "difference principle."

The so-called Paretian Liberal Paradox and other difficulties in aggregating individual preferences cannot be solved on the basis of information provided by the self-interested preferences of individuals. In the evaluation of states of affairs, deontological and stakeholder perspectives should also be used in order to broaden the information base for the evaluation of the state of affairs.

In prisoner's dilemma situations, if each agent pursues her/his self-interest, the result will be suboptimal solutions. In light of the responsible-choice model, the cooperative and noncooperative strategies can be reevaluated. Responsible agents who evaluate the strategies from multiple perspectives can arrive at optimal, that is, multiply satisficing solutions.

Cost-benefit analyses can provide misleading results if environmental and social externalities are present and a high degree of uncertainty is involved. In such cases monetary evaluation of the state of affairs is not enough, no matter how sophisticated the applied procedure of assessing costs and benefits is in monetary terms. The state of affairs should also be evaluated from the ecological and social points of view. The maximin rule implies that a project is worthy of being undertaken if the worst aspect of the state of affairs with the project is better than the worst aspect of the state of affairs without the project.

The ethical performance of a business organization can be determined by evaluating its activities from the perspective of the applying ethical norms. The social performance of a business organization can be determined by evaluating its impacts on the stakeholders. Profit-generating activities of a business organization are acceptable if they do not violate the relevant ethical norms and cause no harm to the stakeholders. Hence nonviolence emerges as a necessary and sufficient condition for the ethical and social acceptability of profit making.

Any economic arrangement affects nature, society and future generations. An economic arrangement is hardly legitimate if it produces negative payoffs for these primordial stakeholders. Justice among nature, society and future generations is established if the economic arrangement produces approximately equal values for nature, society and future generations. This may lead to an extension of the biblical adage to the form, "Love Nature and Future Generations as your own Society."

Complex choice situations require multiperspective considerations. The crux of the matter is how the evaluative space of decision making is defined. The informational basis of business and public decision making should be extended to include ethical, social and ecological values.

The universal substitutability of values propagated by mainstream economics should be challenged. The quality of life can be preserved and enhanced if decision makers pay equal attention to all the relevant value perspectives in the decision situation. The maximin rule permits only limited tradeoffs among different values to keep life as diverse and complex as possible. Responsible decision making is not a luxury; rather, it is a precondition of life worthy to live.

One may think that the maximin rule used in the responsible decision making model is just not good enough today. Given the worsening trends of inhabitation on the planet and unchecked proclivity of humanity, it can be doubted that compromising ourselves for the least worst of the choices will mean a sustainable future for humanity. It is true that the maximin rule does not necessarily produce a desirable outcome in any given situation. However, it is aimed at achieving practically feasible and ethical solutions in complex choice situations where there are multiple conflicts among the ethical norms, the decision makers' goals and the interests of the stakeholders. In many real world cases arriving at more desirable solutions requires redesigning the whole system in which the decision should be made. But this problematic is beyond the scope of a study about responsible decision making.

The Appendices of the book push things forward. They focus on the implementation of environmental principles in the European Union and alternative globalization strategies of multinational companies.

2. The Idea of Moral Responsibility

In this chapter the idea of responsibility will be discussed in depth. In Section 2.1 choice situations are classified. In complex choice situations, the choice has wide-ranging consequences, and other parties in addition to the decision maker can be affected by the outcome of the choice.

In Section 2.2 different uses of the term "responsibility" are discussed. The term may be used in a causal, rule-following or decision-making context. The contrast between prospective and retrospective responsibility is emphasized. It is argued that personal responsibility can be projected to collective responsibility, so organizations are claimed to be responsible in the same way individuals are held responsible.

In Section 2.3 Hans Jonas' famous "Imperative of Responsibility" is presented. Jonas promotes prospective moral responsibility as a response to the challenges of modern technology. He defines responsibility as a nonreciprocal duty to care for all living beings including human persons, nonhuman creatures and future generations.

In Section 2.4 Carol Gilligan's ethic of care is presented, which has important similarities with Jonas' idea of responsibility.

2.1 Complex Choice Situations

To address the problem of responsibility properly, we first need to make some classification of human choice situations. Jon Elster offers such a classification, and it is simple but powerful. His criteria are the importance of the problem and the number of agents involved (Elster, J. 1990: pp. 39-40).

"Small" problems are problems in which the alternatives do not differ much from each other in value. Either the options are equally good or it is not clear that it would pay to find out which is better. In the case of "large" problems, the choice has wide-ranging consequences—for example, decisions spanning big chunks of life involving events in the distant future.

Decisions involving one agent and decisions involving many agents are strikingly different. One-agent problems have no strategic indeterminacy, whereas multiagent problems present much indeterminacy concerning the outcome to be realized.

I refer to large problems with more than one agent as complex choice situations. As mentioned above, in such situations the choice has wide-ranging consequences that affect other parties in addition to the decision maker. This book deals with complex choice situations.

Consider the following three cases that illustrate the nature of complex choice situations. The cases are analyzed in detail in Chapter 8 of the book.

The Case of Donna

Ali is an East African shopkeeper in London who is hated by a small group of racists. A particular gang of them is planning to beat Ali on an evening when Ali goes home. Donna, a West Indian friend of Ali, has just come to hear of the plan and wants to warn Ali about it. Donna does not know where Ali is, but she does know that he has left a message with his business contact, Charles, about his movements. Charles is away for the day also, and the only way of getting Ali's message is by breaking into Charles' room.

Donna can certainly frustrate the planned beating of Ali, but she cannot do this without violating the privacy of Charles, who is both a secretive man and a self-centered egoist. He will be more frustrated by the violation of his privacy than by the beating of Ali. What should Donna do in such a situation? (Sen, A. 1982).

The Ford Pinto Case

In 1978 three girls died in Winamac, Indiana because their Ford Pinto car exploded. This was not the first case in which this particular Ford model caused serious accidents due to explosion. There were lawsuits filed against Ford after it was proven that the top managers of the company had previously been informed about the design problem of the model. Despite the warnings of the engineers, Ford management decided to manufacture and sell the car (Hoffman, M.W. 1984).

The World Bank Case

In 1991 Lawrence Summers, chief economist at the World Bank, explored the idea that the World Bank should be encouraging more migration of dirty industries to less-developed countries. The economic argument is that this policy would enhance global welfare. Should the World Bank adopt such a policy? (Hausman, D.M. & McPherson, M.S. 1996).

2.2 Differing Types of Responsibility

The term "responsibility" is used in different ways in various contexts. A formal model might be helpful in distinguishing among the meanings and references of the term (Kirschenmann, P.P. 1991: p. 97).

"Being responsible" is basically a three-place relation: *X* is responsible for 7 to Z. Here "*X*" refers to the subject of responsibility, who can be an individual or a collectivity. "7" refers to the object of responsibility, which can be an action, the consequences of an action, a policy, a task, or a person to be taken care of, etc. Finally, "*Z*" refers to an authority to which the subject is accountable. This might be a god, an institution, one's own conscience, a society, humankind or the like.

A further referential element is the time at which the subject *X* is responsible. This can be before or after the object 7 obtains. Another referential element consists in the grounds on which the subject *X* is responsible. These can consist of various sorts of criteria—principles or values, an agreement, a contract or role, etc.

Kenneth E. Goodpaster differentiates among three contexts in which the term "responsibility" is used quite regularly. He refers to these uses as causal, rule-following, and decision-making (Goodpaster, K.E. 1983: pp. 4-5).

In the causal use of the term, an actor is responsible if a certain action or event was wholly or in part caused by the action of that particular actor: Thus, for example, we might ask who was responsible for a broken window, to identify the individual or individuals in question. In the causal sense, we are concerned with determining such matters as intent, free will, degree of participation, as well as reward and/or punishment.

In the rule-following use of the term, we focus our attention not on determining who or what brought about a certain action or event, but on the socially expected behavior associated with certain roles. In this sense "parents have responsibilities for their children, doctors for their patients, lawyers for their clients, and citizens for their country." To speak of actors as being responsible in the rule-following context is essentially to commend them for following the rules or meeting the expectations of their stations.

There is a third use of the term that is distinct from both the causal and rule-following ones—the decision-making sense of responsibility, which relates to the way in which an actor thinks about and responds to choice situations. "When we say of Bill Jones that he is a responsible person, we convey that he is reliable and trustworthy, that he can be depended upon to interpret situations and take actions that manifest both integrity and concern for those affected by them."

Another important distinction exists between prospective responsibility and retrospective responsibility (Zimmerman, M. J. 1992).

To bear prospective responsibility for something means that the actor has a duty or obligation to assure that that thing occurs or obtains. In this sense the lifeguard is responsible for the swimmers' safety, which means that it is the lifeguard's duty to ensure the swimmers' safety. Here the actor's responsibility is ex ante in nature because that for which he or she is responsible lies in the future.

Retrospective responsibility is quite different. Here the actor's responsibility is ex post; that is, the actor is responsible for that which lies in the past, not the future. In this sense the lifeguard might be responsible for a swimmer's death as opposed to the protection of a swimmer's life. However, retrospective responsibility may be positive rather than negative. In this case it is tantamount to a sort of praiseworthiness rather than blameworthiness, as when a generous donor is said to be responsible for a charity's success.

This book deals with prospective moral responsibility in a decision-making context. It is what use of the term "moral responsibility" refers to from this point forward.

Moral responsibility necessarily emerges in complex choice situations where the choice has wide ranging consequences that can ultimately affect other parties as well as the decision maker.

I do not emphasize the usual distinction between personal responsibility and collective responsibility. This distinction does not make a difference if we accept the argument of Kenneth E. Goodpaster, according to which the basic characteristics of personal responsibility can be projected to collective responsibility (especially where organizations are concerned).

The principle of moral projection is as follows: "It is appropriate not only to describe organizations (and their characteristics) by analogy with individuals, it is also appropriate normatively to look for and to foster moral attributes in organizations by analogy with those we look for and foster in individuals" (Goodpaster, K.E. 1983: p. 10.).

Simply speaking, the principle of moral projection says that we can and should expect no more and no less of our institutions as moral units than we expect of ourselves as individuals. So in exploring moral responsibility, it is not necessary to differentiate between individual persons and collectivities. The normative model of ethical decision making can be applied to both types of moral agents.

2.3 Hans Jonas' Idea of "Caring for Beings"

In the philosophical literature, a lot of work has been done on retrospective moral responsibility (Fisher, J. [ed.] 1986; Fisher, J.M. & Ravizza, M. [eds.] 1993; Frankfurt, H.G. 1988; Lucas, R.J. 1995; Zimmerman, M.J. 1988). However, only a few works are available on prospective moral responsibility, which is our primary concern in this book.

The most comprehensive theory of prospective moral responsibility is presented by the German-American philosopher Hans Jonas in his opus magnum *The Imperative of Responsibility* (Jonas, H. 1979, 1984).

Jonas was born in Germany in 1903. He was tutored under the guidance of Edmund Husserl, Martin Heidegger, and Rudolf Bultmann. Jonas began his philosophical work on the subject of Gnosticism, and its role in the late Antiquity (Bernstein, R.J. 1995).

In 1933 he emigrated from Hitler's Germany. During the Second World War he served as soldier in the British Underground for several years. Later he became an artillery officer in the Israeli Army (1948).

Jonas wrote the following about his war experience:

> I had to stop work on the Gnostic project per force. But something more substantive and essential was involved. The apocalyptic state of things, the threatening collapse of the world, the climactic crisis of civilization, the proximity of death, the stark nakedness to which all the issues of life were stripped, all these were grounds enough to take a new look at the very foundations of our being and to review the principles by which we guide our thinking on them (Jonas, H.I 974: p. xii).

In the postwar period the phenomenon of life became Jonas' main philosophical concern. He had been questioning the Cartesian dualism of mind and matter. This led Jonas to the conclusion "that the organism with its insoluble fusion of inwardness and outwardness constituted the crucial counterevidence to the dualistic division and, by our privileged experimental access to it, the prime paradigm for philosophy of concrete, uncurtailed being—indeed the key to a reintegration of fragmented ontology into a uniform theory of being" (Jonas, H. 1974: p. xiii).

Jonas taught philosophy at The New School for Social Research for many years. Later he became associated with The Hastings Center in New York, where his main preoccupation was addressing issues of biomedical ethics, especially those related to death and dying.

Jonas' book *The Phenomenon of Life: Toward a Philosophical Biology* was the culmination of his thought on life and living beings (Jonas, H. 1966). In the epilogue of his book Jonas announces a new task for research: Considering the "continuity of mind with organism, and organism with nature, ethics becomes part of the philosophy of nature. (...) Only an ethics which is grounded in the breadth of being (...) can have significance in the scheme of things."

The development of such an ethical theory, the ethics responsibility, was at the forefront of Jonas' thinking for the remainder of his life. He died at age ninety in 1993.

Jonas published the German version of his theory of responsibility in 1979 under the title *Das Prinzip Verantwortung. Versuch einer Ethic fur die Technologische Zivilization* (Jonas, H. 1979). The rewritten and enlarged English edition was published in 1984 under the title *The Imperative of Responsibility: In Search of an Ethics for the Technological Age* (Jonas, H. 1984).

Jonas' theory can be considered a response to Martin Heidegger's famous essay "The Question Concerning Technology" (Heidegger, M. 1977). As Bernstein writes:

> Heidegger too seeks to make us aware of the supreme danger of the essence of modern technology, *Gestell,* which turns everything into "standing reserve" and even human beings into "human resources." What is lacking in Heidegger's analysis—from Jonas' perspective—is an "ethics of responsibility." Jonas affirms as primordial and central precisely what Heidegger denies—that a new ethics can be metaphysically grounded, indeed grounded in a more adequate theory of being where nature itself affirms the ought-to-be of life. Nevertheless, Jonas' model for "the primordial phenomenon of responsibility" is very close to Heidegger's understanding of care (*Sorge*) (Bernstein, R.J. 1995: p. 17).

Jonas' theory of responsibility has not been fully elaborated. However, as he emphasized in his last public lecture, there can be no end to rethinking responsibility (Jonas, H. 1994).

In his opus magnum Jonas' basic preoccupation is with the impact of modern technology on the human condition. The major theses on which his theory of responsibility is based are as follows:

(i) "The altered, always enlarged nature of human action, with the magnitude and novelty of its works and their impact on man's global future."

(ii) "Responsibility is a correlate of power and must be commensurate with the latter's scope and that of its exercise."

(iii) "An imaginative 'heuristics of fear', replacing the former projections of hope, must tell us what is possibly at stake and what we must beware of."

(iv) "Metaphysics must underpin ethics. Hence, a speculative attempt is made at such an underpinning of man's duties toward himself, his distant posterity, and the plenitude of life under his dominion."

(v) "Objective imperatives for man in the scheme of things enable us to discriminate between legitimate and illegitimate goal-settings to our Promethean power" (Jonas, H. 1984: p. x).

Jonas argues that the nature of human action has changed so dramatically in our times that it calls for a radical change in ethics as well.

He emphasizes that in previous ethics,

> all dealing with the nonhuman world, that is, the whole realm of *techne* (...) was ethically neutral. (...) Ethical significance belonged to the direct dealing of man with man, including man dealing with himself: all traditional ethics is *anthropocentric.* (...) The entity of "man" and his basic condition was considered constant in essence and not itself an object of reshaping *techne.* (...) The effective range of action was small, the time span of foresight, goal-setting, and accountability was short, control of circumstances limited (Jonas, H. 1984: pp. 4-5).

According to Jonas new dimensions of responsibility emerged because nature became a subject of human responsibility. This is underlined by the fact of the irreversibility and cumulative character of man's impact on the living world. Knowledge, under these circumstances, is a prime duty of man and must be commensurate with the causal scale of human action. Man should seek "not only the human good but also the good of things extra human, that is, to extend the recognition of 'ends in themselves' beyond the sphere of man and make the human good include the care of them" (Jonas, H. 1984: pp. 7-8).

For Jonas an imperative responding to the new type of human action might run like this, "Act so that the effects of your action are compatible with the permanence of genuine human life," Or, expressed negatively, "Act so that the effects of your action are not destructive of the future possibility of such life" (Jonas, H. 1984: p. 11).

Because future human beings and nonhuman beings do not have rights, our duties to future generations and to nature are independent of any idea of a right or reciprocity. Jonas states that human responsibility is basically a nonreciprocal duty to guard beings (Jonas, H. 1984: pp. 38-39).

Like physicist Friedrich von Weizschecker (1971) and deep ecologist Arne Naess (1989), Jonas argues for an objectivity of values regarding the purposefulness of living beings:

> Nature, by entertaining ends, or having aims, as we now assume her to do, also posits values. For with any *de facto* pursued end (...) attainment of it becomes a good, and frustration of it, an evil; and with this distinction the attributability of value begins.(...) We can regard the mere *capacity* to *have* any purposes at all as a good-in-itself, of which we grasp with the intuitive certainty that it is infinitely superior to any purposelessness of being (Jonas, H. 1984: pp. 79-80).

Purpose has its own accreditation within being. This is an ontological axiom for Jonas that lies on the following:

> [An] ultimate metaphysical choice, which can give no further account of itself. (...) We can see a fundamental self-affirmation of being, which posits it *absolutely* as the better over a non-being. (...) Hence, the mere fact that being is not indifferent toward itself makes its difference from non-being the basic value of all, the first "yes" in general. (...) Self-affirmation of being becomes emphatic in the opposition of life to death (Jonas, H. 1984: pp. 80-81).

Jonas states that the necessary conditions of moral responsibility are as follows: "The first and most general condition of responsibility is causal power, that is, that acting makes an impact on the world; the second, that such acting is under the agent's control; and the third, that he can foresee its consequences to some extent" (Jonas, H. 1984: p. 90).

Jonas underlines the fact that prospective responsibility is never formal but always substantive. "I feel responsible, not in the first place for my conduct and its consequences but for the matter that has a claim on my acting." For example "the well-being, the interest, the fate of others has, by circumstance or by agreement, come to my care, which means that my control *over* it involves at the same time my obligation *for* it" (Jonas, H. 1984: p. 92 and p. 93).

Jonas differentiates between natural responsibility on the one hand and contractual responsibility on the other: "It is the distinction between natural responsibility, where the immanent 'ought-to-be' of the object claims its agent a priori and quite unilaterally, and contracted or appointed responsibility, which is conditional a posteriori upon the fact and the terms of the relationship actually entered into" (Jonas, H. 1984: p. 95).

The parent and the statesman are presented as ideal types of natural responsibility and contractual responsibility, respectively. Concerning their responsibility, the roles of parent and statesman have much in common. These common features are totality, continuity, and future-orientation:

> Responsibilities encompass the total being of their object. (...) The pure being as such, and then the best being of the child, is what parental care is about. (...) [The statesman's responsibility,] for duration of his office or his power, is for the total life of community, the "public weal." (...) Neither parental nor governmental care can allow itself a vacation or pause, for the life of the object continues without intermission, making its demands anew, time after time. More important still is the continuity of the cared-for *existence* itself as a *concern.* (...) It is the future with which responsibility for a life, be it individual or communal, is concerned beyond its immediate present. (...) An agent's *concrete* moral *responsibility* at the time of action does extend further than to its proximate effects (Jonas, H. 1984: p. 102, p. 105 and p. 107).

Jonas summarizes the imperative of responsibility as follows: "The concept of responsibility implies that of an ought—first of an ought-to-be of something, then of an ought-to-do of someone in response to the first." This is most evident in the case of a newborn baby "whose mere breathing uncontradictably addresses an ought to the world around, namely, to take care of him." Not only the newborn calls us in this way, but so does "the unconditional end-in-itself of everything alive and the still-have-to-come of the faculties for securing this end" (Jonas, H. 1984: p. 130 and p. 134).

2.4 The Moral Experience of Women

There are similarities between Jonas' theory of responsibility and the ethic of care described by Carol Gilligan in her best-selling book *In a Different Voice: Psychological Theory and Women's Development* (Gilligan, C. 1982).

Conducting empirical studies at Harvard on the moral experience of women, Gilligan found that the morality of women is strikingly different from the morality of men: "Relationships, and particularly issues of dependency, are experienced differently by women and men. (...) The quality of embeddedness in social interaction and personal relationships that characterize women's lives in contrast to men's" (Gilligan, C. 1982: pp. 8-9).

Gilligan characterizes the morality of women as an ethic of care. "The ideal of care is thus an activity of relationship, of seeing and responding to need, taking care of the world by sustaining the web of connection so that no one is left alone." The ethic of care "is the wish not to hurt others and the hope that in morality lies a way of solving conflicts so that no one will be hurt." Women consider the inflicting of hurt as "selfish and immoral in its reflection of unconcern, while the expression of care is seen as fulfillment of moral responsibility" (Gilligan, C. 1982: p. 62, p. 65, and p. 73).

Identity is defined differently by women and men. For women "identity is defined in a context of relationship and judged by a standard of responsibility and care. (...) Morality stems from attachment." For men "the tone of identity is different, clearer, more distinct and sharp-edged. (...) Thus the male T is defined in separation" (Gilligan, C. 1982: pp. 160-161).

Gilligan states that men and women represent two different moral ideologies: the ethic of rights and the ethic of care, respectively.

Separation is justified by an ethic of rights while attachment is supported by an ethic of care:

> The morality of rights is predicated on equality and centered on the understanding of fairness, while the ethic of responsibility relies on the concept of equity, the recognition of differences in need. While the ethic of rights is a

manifestation of equal respect, balancing the claims of other and the self, the ethic of responsibility rests on an understanding that gives rise to compassion and care (Gilligan, C.1982: p. 165).

Table 2 shows the contrasting features of male and female morality.

TABLE 2
Male Morality versus Female Morality

Male morality	Female morality
separation	attachment
focus on rights	focus on needs
indifference	nonviolence
justice	care
equality	equity
individual achievement	sustaining relationships

Gilligan does not argue for the superiority of women's morality. She emphasizes the complementarity of male and female ethics: "We arrive at a more complex rendition of human experience which sees the truth of separation and attachment in the lives of women and men and recognizes how these truths are carried by different modes of languages and thought" (Gilligan, C. 1982: p. 174).

The two disparate modes of moral experience are connected in mature morality:

> While an ethic of justice proceeds from the premise of equality—that everyone should be treated the same—an ethic of care rests on the premise of non-violence—that no one should be hurt. (...) [In maturity] both perspectives converge in the realization that just as inequality adversely affects both parties in an unequal relationship, so too violence is destructive for everyone involved (Gilligan, C. 1982: p. 174).

The ethic of rights and the ethic of care possibly reflect evolutionarily stable strategies. Both strategies are viable and have their own worth. The early Chinese Yin & Yang polarity predicates that both male and female principles are necessary for the health and good functioning of the microcosmos as well as the macrocosmos (Capra, F. 1981).

For a man "responsibility means not doing what he wants because he is thinking of others." Contrary to this, for a woman "responsibility means doing what others are counting on her to do regardless of what she herself wants" (Gilligan, C. 1982: p. 38). An advanced concept of responsibility should integrate the reverence for rights represented by men and the nonviolence of care represented by women.

2.5 Summary

Large decision problems with more than one agent present complex choice situations. In such situations responsibility is unavoidable because the choice has wide-ranging consequences and the outcomes affect both the decision maker and other parties.

"Being responsible" is basically a three-place relation: X is responsible for 7 to Z where "X" refers to the subject of responsibility, "Y" refers to the object of responsibility, and finally, "Z" refers to an authority to which the subject is accountable. A further element is the time at which the subject X is responsible. This can be before or after the object Y obtains. Another element consists in the grounds on which the subject X is responsible.

We should differentiate among contexts in which the term "responsibility" is used. In the causal use of the term, an actor is responsible if a certain action or event was wholly or in part caused by the action of that particular actor. In the rule-following use of the term, we focus our attention not on determining who or what brought about a certain action or event, but on the socially expected behavior associated with certain roles. Finally, there is the decision-making sense of responsibility that relates to the way in which an actor thinks about and responds to choice situations.

The final important distinction is made when we contrast prospective responsibility with retrospective responsibility. To bear prospective responsibility for something means that the actor has a duty or obligation to assure that that thing occurs or obtains. Retrospective responsibility means that the actor's responsibility is ex post facto; or, that for which the actor is responsible lies in the past, not in the future.

When exploring moral responsibility, it is not necessary to differentiate between individual persons and collectivities. The normative model of responsibility can be applied to both types of moral agents.

The most comprehensive theory of prospective moral responsibility is presented by the German-American philosopher, Hans Jonas in his opus magnum *The Imperative of Responsibility.* Jonas argues that the nature of human action has changed so dramatically in our times that it calls for a radical change in ethics as well.

According to Jonas new dimensions of responsibility emerged because nature became a subject of human responsibility. This is underlined by the irreversibility and cumulative character of man's impact on the living world. Knowledge, under these circumstances, is a prime duty of man and must be commensurate with the causal scale of human action.

For Jonas an imperative responding to the new type of human action might run like this, "Act so that the effects of your action are compatible with the permanence of genuine human life." Or, expressed negatively, "Act so that the effects of your action are not destructive of the future possibility of such life." Since future human beings and nonhuman beings do not have rights, our duties to future generations and to nature are independent of any idea of a right or reciprocity. Human responsibility is basically a nonreciprocal duty to guard beings.

Jonas differentiates between natural responsibility on the one hand and contractual responsibility on the other. The parent and the statesman are presented as ideal types of natural responsibility and contractual responsibility, respectively. Concerning their responsibility, the roles of parent and statesman have much in common. These common features are totality, continuity, and future-orientation.

Jonas summarizes the imperative of responsibility as follows: "The concept of responsibility implies that of an ought—first of an ought-to-be of something, then of an ought-to-do of someone in response to the first." This is most evident in the case of a newborn baby "whose mere breathing uncontradictably addresses an ought to the world around, namely, to take care of him." Not only the newborn calls us in this way but so does "the unconditional end-in-itself of everything alive and the still-have-to-come of the faculties for securing this end."

There are important similarities between Jonas 'theory of responsibility and the ethic of care described by Carol Gilligan. Gilligan characterizes the morality of women as the ethic of care. "The ideal of care is thus an activity of relationship, of seeing and responding to need, taking care of the world by sustaining the web of connection so that no one is left alone." The ethic of care "is the wish not to hurt others and the hope that in morality lies a way of solving conflicts so that no one will be hurt." Women consider the inflicting of hurt as "selfish and immoral in its reflection of unconcern, while the expression of care is seen as fulfillment of moral responsibility."

Gilligan states that men and women represent two different moral ideologies: the ethic of rights and the ethic of care, respectively.

The ethic of rights and the ethic of care possibly reflect two distinct but evolutionarily stable strategies of men and women. Both strategies are viable and have their own worth. The early Chinese Yin & Yang polarity depicts both male and female principles as necessary for the health and good functioning of the microcosmos as well as the macrocosmos. An advanced concept of responsibility should integrate the reverence for rights represented by men and the nonviolence of care represented by women.

3. Criticizing Rational Choice

In this chapter the rational choice model will be introduced and discussed. Various criticisms of the model will be recalled from different disciplines such as psychology, sociology, and economics, as well as from different perspectives such as communitarianism, environmentalism and feminism.

In Section 3.1 the rational choice model is stated accurately using some symbolic representation.

In Section 3.2 Herbert A. Simon's, theory of bounded rationality is presented. In Section 3.3 experimental results are reported that reveal serious obstacles to maximizing utility. In Section 3.4 the most famous cases are recalled in which people systematically violate the axioms of the expected utility theory.

In Section 3.5 Amartya Sen's powerful criticism is presented of both the consistency view of rationality and the view of rationality as self-interest. In Section 3.6 Robert Frank's model is introduced, which shows the strategic role of emotions in human choice behavior.

In Section 3.7 Jon Elster's theory of social norms, where norm-guided behavior is described in terms other than self-interest maximizing, is covered.

In Section 3.8 communitarian and environmental criticisms of the rational choice model are presented. Amitai Etzioni's "I & We" paradigm, which represents a balancing view over utility and morality, is discussed.

In Section 3.9 Jane Mansbridge's tripartite scheme of duty, self-interest, and love is presented. Human behavior is understood as being determined by these irreducible motives in an intermingled way.

3.1 The Rational Choice Model

The rational choice model has been widely used in economics, political science and other social sciences as a basic model of human choice behavior. The model states that in order to be considered rational, the agent should maximize his or her utility function.

Under the circumstances of complete certainty, a more accurate formulation of the model is as follows: Agents are rational if their preferences are rational and they choose what they most prefer among the available alternatives (Hausmann, D.M. & McPherson, M.S. 1996: pp. 27-28).

Transitivity and completeness are necessary and sufficient conditions of the rationality of preferences.

Let **A** be an agent and **x, y,** and **z** be different alternatives available to her/him. **A**'s preferences are transitive in the case

$$\text{if } x \longrightarrow y \text{ and } y \longrightarrow z \text{ then } x \longrightarrow z \qquad (3.1)$$

and

$$\text{if } x \longleftrightarrow y \text{ and } x \longleftrightarrow z \text{ then } x \longleftrightarrow z \qquad (3.2)$$

(3.1) and (3.2) mean that if **A** prefers **x** to **y** and **y** to **z** then she or he prefers **x** to **y**. Similarly, if **A** is indifferent between **x** and **y**, and between **x** and **z**, then she or he is indifferent between **x** and **z**.

A's preferences are complete in the case

$$x \longrightarrow y \text{ or } x \longleftarrow y \text{ or } x \longleftrightarrow y \qquad (3.3)$$

(3.3) means that for all alternatives, **A** prefers **x** to **y** or **y** to **x**, or **A** is indifferent between **x** and **y**.

Completeness and transitivity together establish a weak ordering of the finite set of alternatives. One can assign numbers to the alternatives in a way that preferred alternatives always get higher numbers while indifferent alternatives always get the same number. Any such assignment of numbers forms an ordinal utility function. "Utility" here does not refer specifically to usefulness or pleasure. A utility function is only a way representing the preference ranking of an agent (Hausman, D.M. & McPherson, M.S. 1996: pp. 28-29).

In circumstances of certainty, the rational choice model can be restated as follows: An agent is rational if and only if her or his preferences may be accurately represented by an ordinal utility function, and her or his choices are utility maximizing ones.

In circumstances of risk and uncertainty, the rational choice model is formulated within the framework of the expected utility theory. The expected utility theory considers actions to be lotteries when actions do not lead with certainty to any particular outcome. To be rational, the agent's preferences among lotteries must be transitive, complete, and continuous. However, a further condition is also required, namely independence. The theory says that if two lotteries differ only in one prize, then the actor's preference between the lotteries should match her or his preferences between the prizes. If the agent's preferences satisfy all the above requirements, then they can be represented by a cardinal utility function (Hausman, D.M. & McPherson, M.S. 1996: pp. 30-31).

The cardinal utility function has the so-called expected utility property that states that the expected utility of a lottery is equal to the utilities of its outcomes multiplied by the corresponding probabilities.

Let **G** be a gain and **L** be a loss for an agent. Suppose that she or he will get **G** with probability **p(G)** and **L** with probability **p(L).** Let **U(G)** and **U(L)** be the utilities of **G** and **L** for the agent, respectively. In this case, the expected utility of such a lottery is the weighted sum of the utilities using probabilities as weights.

$$\mathbf{U(G \; \& \; L) = p(G)U(G) + p(L)U(G)} \qquad (3.4)$$

The cardinal utility function is unique up to a positive affine or linear transformation.

Let **U** be a cardinal utility function and **U'** another one.

$$\mathbf{U' = aU + b} \qquad (3.5)$$

If **a** is a positive real number and **b** is any real number, then **U** and **U'** are doing equally well in representing the preference ordering of the agent.

The rational choice model presupposes nothing about the preferences people have. They may have self-centered preferences, altruistic preferences or even sadomasochistic preferences. The rational choice model represents a formal theory that says nothing about what people prefer or should prefer. Hereafter I refer to this model as the weak form of rationality.

In both economics and political science, we can find a much stronger version of rationality, where the assumptions of self-interest and perfect knowledge are added to the weak form of rationality. Hence we get the well-known "Homo Oeconomicus" model according to which individuals are rational, exclusively self-interested and have perfect knowledge about the consequences of their choices.

The Homo Oeconomicus model does have substantive assumptions about what people want and the manner in which they want it. I refer to this model hereafter as the strong form of rationality.

3.2 Bounded Rationality

Economist and psychologist Herbert A. Simon was a relentless critic of the rational choice model for decades. He states that the model has claims on human beings that are too strong. Real people have poor cognitive capacity and the information available to them is rather limited in most cases.

Agents in the real world are not capable of maximizing their utility function (if they have any). Instead of maximizing, they usually make "satisficing" decisions. They usually choose the first available alternative that is "good enough" for them in the sense that it satisfies their immediate aspiration level. This is the main message of the theory of bounded rationality, for which Simon received the Nobel Prize in Economics in 1978 (Simon, H.A. 1982).

Simon writes the following synopsis of bounded rationality:

> Faced with a choice situation where it is impossible to optimize, or where the computational cost of doing so seems burdensome, the decision maker may look for a satisfactory, rather than an optimal alternative. Frequently, a course of action satisfying a number of constraints, even a sizeable number, is far easier to discover than a course of action maximizing some function (Simon, H.A. 1987: p. 244).

The question arises of how a decision maker may set the level of criteria that define "satisfactory":

> Psychology proposes the mechanism of aspiration levels: if it turns out to be very easy to find alternatives that meet the criteria, the standards are gradually raised:

if the search continues for a long while without finding satisfactory alternatives, the standards are gradually lowered. Thus, by a kind of feedback mechanism, or "tatonement," the decision maker converges toward a set of criteria that are attainable, but not without effort. The difference between the aspiration level mechanism and the optimization procedure is that the former calls for much simpler computations than the latter (Simon, H.A. 1987: p. 244).

During the last few decades, abundant empirical evidence has been produced by economists and psychologists showing that bounded rationality is important in real world situations. Economists who include bounded rationality in their models have excellent success in describing economic behavior beyond the coverage of standard economic theory (Conlisk, J. 1996).

3.3 Myopic and Deficient Choices

Psychologist Daniel Kahneman criticizes the rational choice model on the basis of experimental research. Experimental results indicate that people are myopic in their decisions, may lack skill in predicting their future tastes, and can be led to erroneous choices by fallible memory and the incorrect evaluation of past experiences (Kahneman, D. 1994).

Kahneman differentiates between experienced utility and predicted utility. The experienced utility of an outcome is the measure of the hedonic experience of that outcome. The predicted utility of an outcome is defined as the individual's beliefs about its experienced utility at some future time. Predicted utility is an "ex ante" variable, while experienced utility is an "ex post" variable in the decision-making process. According to the rational choice model, decisions are made on the basis of predicted utility. If experienced utility greatly differs from predicted utility then this may lead to subrational, or even irrational choices.

The problem of predicted utility raises the question, "Do people know what they will like?" Kahneman's answer is a definite "No." The accuracy of people's hedonic predictions is generally quite poor. Experimental studies suggest two conclusions: (i) people may have little ability to forecast changes in their hedonic responses to stimuli; and (ii) even in situations that permit accurate hedonic predictions, people may tend to make decisions about future consumption without due consideration of possible changes in their tastes. (Kahneman, D. 1994: p. 27).

Discrepancies between retrospective utility and real-time utility should also be addressed. This leads to the question, "Do people know what they *have* liked?" Kahneman's answer is again a definite "No." Psychological experiments show that retrospective evaluations should be viewed with greater distrust than introspective reports of current experience. The results of these studies support two empirical generalizations:

> *(1) The Peak & End Rule:* global evaluations are predicted with high accuracy by a weighted combination of the most extreme affect recorded during the episode and of the affect recorded during the terminal moments of the episode.
> *(2) Duration Neglect.* The retrospective evaluation of overall or total pain (or pleasure) is not affected by the duration period (Kahneman, D. 1994: p. 29).

Since individuals use their evaluative memories to guide choices among future outcomes, deceptive retrospective evaluations may lead to erroneous choices.

Kahneman identifies two major obstacles to the maximization of experienced utility required by the rational choice model:

> First, people lack skill in the task of predicting how their tastes might change. (...) It is difficult to describe as rational agents who are prone to large errors in predicting what they will want or enjoy next week. Another obstacle is a tendency to use the affect associated with particular moments as a proxy for the utility of extended outcomes. (...) Observations of memory biases are significant because the evaluation of the past determines what is learned from it. Errors in the lessons drawn from experience will inevitably be reflected in deficient choices for the future (Kahneman, D. 1994: p. 33).

3.4 Violations of the Axioms

Behavioral decision researchers have conducted a number of experiments that demonstrate that people systematically violate the axioms of the expected utility theory. Here I recall the most famous cases only: the Allais paradox, the Ellsberg's problem, the preference-reversal effect and the framing effect.

The "Allais paradox" deals with the independence axiom of the rational choice model. This axiom requires that the choice between two alternatives depend only on the states in which those alternatives yield different outcomes. For testing the validity of the independence axiom, Nobel laureate French economist Maurice Allais generates the following problem pair (Allais, M. 1953):

Problem (1) Choose between
(A) **$1 million with certainty;**
(B) **$5 million with probability 0.10 &**
$1 million with probability 0.89 &
$0 with probability 0.01

Problem (2) Choose between
(C) **$1 million with probability 0.11 &**
$0 with probability 0.89
(D) **$5 million with probability 0.10 &**
$0 with probability 0.90

The common responses to problems (1) and (2) are **A** and **D**, respectively. However, this violates the independence axiom.

Daniel Kahneman and Amos Tversky replicated the experiment with another problem pair. Their study shows that the enormous amounts of money in the original formulation are not essential (Kahneman, D. and Tversky, A. 1979). The Allais paradox can be explained by the "certainty effect," which means that people usually overweight certainty relative to probabilities less than one (Thaler, R.H. 1991: pp. 139-140.).

The Ellsberg's problem is about expectations. (Ellsberg, D. 1961). The rational choice model states that the utility of an outcome is weighted by its probability. The simplest form of the Ellsberg's problem is as follows:

Problem (3)

There are two urns that contain a large number of red and black balls. You know that **Urn A** has **50 percent** red balls and **50 percent** black balls. Urn B has red and black balls in **unknown proportions.** You will win **$100** if you draw the color ball of your choice from an urn. From which urn would you choose a ball?

The Ellsberg's problem reveals that people facing ambiguity may violate the "expected utility property" required by the rational choice model:

Most subjects express a strict preference for **Urn A** with the known proportion rather than the "ambiguous" **Urn B**. Subjects really admit that they would be indifferent about trying for a red or a black ball from the ambiguous urn, thereby indicating that their subjective probabilities of each are the same and presumably equal to 1/2, which is the known proportion in **Urn A**. Nevertheless, most subjects feel that the ambiguous urn is in some sense riskier (Thaler, R.H. 1991: pp. 140-141.).

The so-called preference-reversal effect was discovered by Sarah Lichtenstein and Paul Slavic. It deals with preference ordering (Lichtenstein, S. and Slovic, P. 1971). The rational choice model assumes that the preferences of the agents are fixed in the sense that they do not change according to the context in which they are revealed. The problem that Lichtenstein and Slovic posed to subjects is as follows:

Problem (4) Choose between

(P bet) **35/36** chance to win **$4**
($ bet) **11/36** chance to win **$16**

Subjects were asked to value each bet by stating the minimum amount they would accept to sell each of the bets if they owned the right to play them (or, alternatively, the maximum amount they would pay to buy the gamble.) Surprisingly, a large proportion of the subjects who preferred "p bet" in the choice task assigned a larger value to the "$ bet" in the judgment task. Thus, (...) preferences depend on the method of elicitation (Thaler, R.H. 1991: pp. 143-144.).

Finally, I present the so-called framing effect described by Amos Tversky and Daniel Kahneman. Here the dominance axiom of rational choice is challenged, the axiom which says that if alternative x is better than alternative y, then x should be preferred to y. The following problems illustrate how the dominance axiom is violated (Tversky, A. and Kahneman, D. 1981).

Problem (5)
Imagine that you face the following pair of concurrent decisions.
Decision (i) Choose between
(A) sure gain of **$240**
(B) **25%** chance to gain **$1,000** and **75%** chance to gain nothing.
Decision (ii) Choose between
(C) sure loss of **$175**
(D) **75%** chance to lose **$1,000** and **25%** chance to lose nothing.

73 percent of the subjects chose the combination **A & D** and only **3 percent** picked the opposite combination **B & C**. However, the combination **B & C** actually dominates the combination **A & D**.

The next problem is a reframed version of problem (5).

Problem (6) Choose between
(E) **25%** chance to win **$240** and **75%** chance to lose **$760**
(F) **25%** chance to win **$250** and **75%** chance to lose $**750**.

Every subject preferred **F** to **E**. Notice that **F = B & C** and **E = A & D**. However, the former combination was strongly dispreferred to the latter combination in the case of Problem (5).

The presented violations of the rational choice model seem to be so fundamental that no hybrid, nearly rational model can possibly capture this type of behavior (Thaler, R.H. 1991: pp. 145-146.).

3.5 Rational Fools

Nobel laureate economist Amartya Sen concluded that if real people behaved in the way that is required of them by the rational choice model then they would act like "rational fools" (Sen, A. 1977). Sen criticizes both the weak and strong forms of rationality. He refers to the weak form as "internal consistency of choice" and to the strong form as "maximization of self-interest."

Sen concludes the following:

> It is hard to believe that internal consistency of choice can itself be an adequate condition of rationality. If a person does exactly the opposite of what would help achieving what he or she would want to achieve, and does this with flawless internal consistency (always choosing exactly the opposite of what will enhance the occurrence of things he or she wants and values), the person can scarcely be seen as rational. (...) Rational choice must demand something at least about the correspondence between what one tries to achieve and how one goes about it (Sen, A. 1987: p. 13).

Sen uses the term "correspondence rationality" to describe the correspondence of choice with the aims and values of the agent. He states that this kind of correspondence must be a necessary condition of rationality, whether or not it is also the sufficient condition. Correspondence rationality might be supplemented by some requirements on the nature of the reflection regarding what the actor should want and value (Sen, A. 1987: pp. 13-14). It might well be arguable that rational behavior must demand some consistency, but consistency itself can hardly be adequate to ensure the rationality of choice. Internal consistency is not a guarantee of a person's rationality.

Rationality as self-interest maximization has additional problems. Sen asks, "Why should it be uniquely rational to pursue one's own self-interest to the exclusion of everything else?" He argues that the self-interest view of rationality

> involves inter alia a firm rejection of the "ethics-based" view of motivation. Trying to do one's best to achieve what one would like to achieve can be a part of rationality, and this can include the promotion of non-self-interested goals which we may value and wish to aim at. To see any departure from self-interest maximization as evidence of irrationality must imply a rejection of the role of ethics in actual decision making (Sen, A. 1987: p. 15).

According to Sen "universal selfishness as actuality may well be false, but universal selfishness as a requirement of rationality is patently absurd" (Sen, A. 1987: p. 16). People have complex motivations, both selfish and selfless, in their economic affairs. In the case of Japan, for example, there is strong empirical evidence that beyond self-interested behavior, duty, loyalty, and goodwill have played a substantial part in Japan's industrial success. What is often called "the Japanese ethos" is certainly hard to fit into any simplified picture of self-interested behavior. Sen claims that "the mixture of selfish and selfless behavior is one of the most important characteristics of group loyalty, and this mixture can be seen in a wide variety of group associations varying from kinship relations and communities to trade unions and economic pressure groups" (Sen, A. 1987: pp. 18-20).

3.6 The Strategic Role of Emotions

Cornell University economist Robert Frank developed a model that emphasizes the role of the emotions in making choices. He uses several empirical generalizations to describe the behavior of people in real choice situations (Frank, R. 1988: pp. 245-255).

(i) People often do not behave as predicted by the self-interest model of choice.

(ii) The reason for irrational behavior is not always that people miscalculate.

(iii) Emotions are often an important motive for irrational behavior.
(iv) Being motivated by emotions is often an advantage.

Frank argues that passions often serve our interest well indeed because we face important problems that are simply unsolvable by rational action. "Emotions often predispose us to behave in ways that are contrary to our narrow interests, and being thus predisposed can be an advantage" (Frank, R. 1988: pp. 4-7).

Material incentives are by no means the only force that governs behavior. Human behavior is directly guided by a complex psychological reward mechanism. Rational calculations are the input for the reward mechanism. "Feelings and emotions, apparently, are the proximate causes of most behavior. (...) The reward theory of behavior tells us that these sentiments can and do compete with feelings that spring from rational calculations about material payoffs" (Frank, R. 1988: pp. 51-53).

The modular-brain theory developed by psychologists and neurobiologists David McClelland, Roger W. Sperry, and Michael Gazzaniga seems to support Frank's ideas. According to the modular theory, the brain is organized into a host of separate modules. Each module has its own capacity for processing information and motivating behavior. Most of these brain modules do not "speak." They simply do not have language capability. Even more importantly, these nonlanguage modules are not equally well connected to the central language module of the brain. Perhaps this is the cause of the seeming disparity between different methods of assessing motivation.

Modular-brain theorists view the language module of the brain as the center of our rational consciousness, obsessed with rationalizing all that we feel and do. However, there is a great deal of information that enters the central nervous system that cannot be accessed by the language module. The modular-brain theory suggests "that when economists talk about maximizing utility, they are really talking about the language module of the left hemisphere, however, it does not account for all of our behavior. (...) The rational utility-maximizing language module of the brain may simply be ill-equipped to deal with many of the most important problems we face" (Frank, R. pp. 205-211).

Frank's main conclusion is that persons directly motivated to pursue their self-interest are often doomed to fail for exactly that reason. Problems can often be solved by persons who have abandoned the quest for maximal material advantage. The emotions that lead people to behave in irrational ways can indirectly lead to greater material well-being (Frank, R. 1988: pp. 258-259).

3.7 Social Norms

After a decade-long preoccupation with the rational choice model, sociologist Jon Elster developed an alternative theory that he calls the theory of social norms (Elster, J. 1983, 1984, 1989). Elster contrasts rational action with norm-guided behavior. Rational action is outcome oriented. Rationality says, "If you want to achieve X, do Y." Elster defines social norms as not outcome-oriented devices. Social norms say "Do X," or "Do not do Y"; or "If you do X, then do Y"; or "Do X if it would be good if everyone did X":

> Rationality is essentially conditional and future-oriented. Its imperatives are hypothetical, that is, conditional on the future outcomes one wants to realize. The imperatives expressed in social norms either are unconditional, or if conditional, are not future-oriented. In the latter case norms make the action dependent on past events or (more rarely) on hypothetical outcomes (Elster, J. 1989: p. 98).

Not all norms are social. There are two conditions for norms to be considered social. First, they must be shared by other people; and second, they must be partly sustained by their approval or disapproval:

> In addition to being supported by the attitudes of other people, norms are sustained by the feelings of embarrassment, anxiety, guilt and shame that a person suffers at the prospect of violating them, or at least at the prospect of being caught violating them. Social norms have a *grip on the mind that* is due to the strong emotions their violations can trigger. (...) A norm, in this perspective, is *the propensity to feel shame and to anticipate sanctions by others at the thought of behaving in a certain, forbidden way* (Elster, J. 1989: pp. 99-100 and p. 105).

Elster argues for the reality and autonomy of social norms. By the reality of norms he means that norms have independent motivating power. Norms do not merely represent an ex post rationalization of self-interest. They serve independently as ex ante sources of action. Autonomy of norms means that they have an irreducibility to optimization (Elster, J. 1989: p. 125). The basic question revolves around the interaction between social norms and self-interested motivations. Elster developed a simplified model for the determinants of human action. (Figure 1).

FIGURE 1
Determinants of Human Action

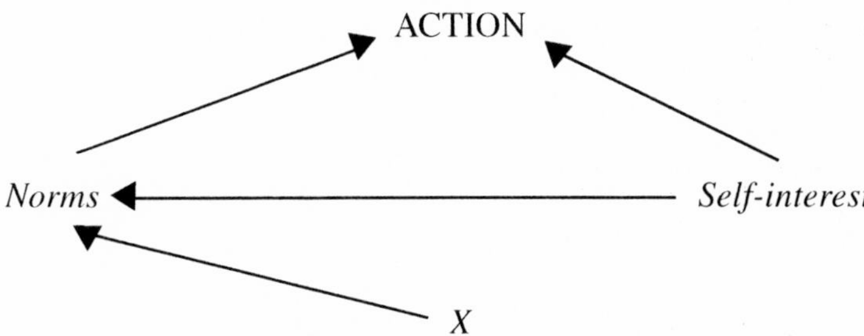

In Elster's model people's actions are determined by *self-interest* and by the *norms* to which they subscribe. Norms are partly shaped by self-interest because people often adhere to the norms that favor them. However, norms are not fully reducible to self-interest. The unknown residual is a brute fact (Elster, J. 1989: p. 150).

3.8 The Communitarian Challenge

Communitarian thinkers forcefully criticize the liberal conception of the self that is at the heart of the rational choice model.

Canadian philosopher Charles Taylor has argued that the liberal conception of the self is basically an atomistic conception of the person and human agency focusing exclusively on will and freedom of choice. This conception is most clearly expressed in Robert Nozick's *Anarchy, State, and Utopia* (Nozick, R. 1974). Taylor defends a relational, inter subjective conception of the self that stresses the social, cultural, historical and linguistic constitution of personal identity. By rejecting the voluntaristic conception of human agency he has formulated a cognitive conception that emphasizes the role of critical reflection, self-interpretation, and rational evaluation (Taylor, C. 1985).

Harvard political scientist Michael Sandel has stressed the constitutive role of community in the formation of identity of persons. He shows the inadequacy and misleading character of the disembedded and unencumbered conception of the self that underlines John Rawls' theory of justice (Rawls, J. 1971). Sandel highlights the cognitive dimensions of reflection and deliberation for an adequate view of human agency (Sandel, M. 1982).

Catholic philosopher Alasdair MacIntyre defends a teleological and contextualist view of human agency. According to him, moral conduct is characterized by the exercise of virtues and aims at realization of the good. No agent can properly locate, interpret, and evaluate her or his actions except by participating in a moral tradition or in a moral community (MacIntyre, A. 1981, 1988).

Communitarian sociologist Amitai Etzioni develops a theory that he calls socio-economics. He introduces the "I & We" paradigm, that "sees individuals as able to act rationally and on their own, advancing their self or T, but their ability to do so is deeply affected by how well they are anchored within a sound community and sustained by a firm moral and emotive personal underpinning—a community they perceive as theirs, as 'We'" (Etzioni, A. 1988: p. x.).

Etzioni presents a new model of decision making in which people's choices are based largely on emotions and value judgments and only secondarily on logical-empirical considerations. In Etzioni's model two irreducible sources of valuations play a role, namely pleasure and morality.

> Individuals are, simultaneously, under the influence of two major sets of factors—their pleasure, and their moral duty (although both reflect socialization). (...) There are important differences in the extent each of these sets of factors is operative under different historical and societal conditions, and within different personalities under the same conditions (Etzioni, A. 1988: p. 63).

The relationship between pleasure and morality is that while both affect choice, they also affect one another. However, each factor is only partially shaped by the other; that is, each factor has a considerable measure of autonomy. This co-determination model is shown by Figure 2.

FIGURE 2
Pleasure and Morality in the Context of Choice

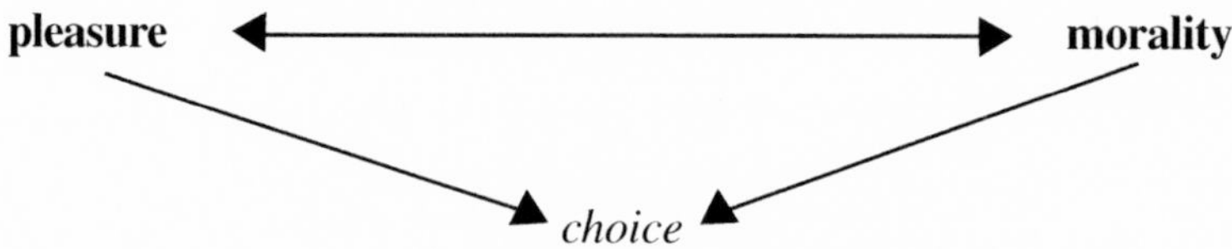

Etzioni states that "people do not seek to maximize their pleasure, but to balance their service of the two major purposes—to advance their well-being and to act morally" (Etzioni, A. 1988: p. 83).

Etzioni breaks with the rationalist framework of choice. He states that the choices of individuals are governed by normative commitments and affective involvements:

> The majority of choices people make, including economic ones, are completely or largely based on normative-affective considerations, not merely with regard to the selection of goals, but also of means. (...) The limited zones in which other, logical-empirical considerations are paramount, are themselves defined by normative-affective factors that legitimate and otherwise motivate such decision-making (Etzioni, A. 1988: p. 93).

The rational choice model can also be criticized from an environmental point of view. It is very questionable that the sustainability of natural systems can be assured on the basis of self-interested individual choices. The I & We paradigm of Etzioni can be enlarged by introducing a third element into it, namely Mother Nature, in which both individuals and collectivities are embedded (Zsolnai, L. 1995).

Humans are biosocial beings. They have emotions linked to the environment and are engaged in environmental values. These values and emotions are expressed in their preferences and moral commitments. Environmental economics has developed a rich variety of methods to reveal the environmental preferences of people (Pearce, D. 1993). One may criticize the methods of environmental economics, but its empirical findings clearly show that people do have environmental preferences. Emotions related to the environment serve as a basis for environmental ethics. Nature can be, and actually is, the subject of various moral commitments (Fox, W. 1990).

At the level of biological creatures, the so-called awareness-based ethics is the most relevant. This states that every sentient being should be respected (at least to some degree). At the level of coexisting populations, the ecosystem ethics appears. The essence of this is that an act is right when it tends to preserve the integrity, stability, and beauty of the biotic community. Finally, at the level of the Earth, a Gaian ethics is emerging which stresses that the global patterns and mechanisms of the biosphere must not be violated or disturbed. People may value nature as a source of utility (economically or in terms of its life-support) and for its own sake or intrinsic value.

3.9 Duty, Self-interest, and Love

In the feminist literature the rational choice theory, and especially the strong form of rationality, is often criticized for presupposing an androcentric, male-biased conception of the human person, the so-called "separative self (England, P. and Stanek Kilbourne, B. 1990; Ferber, M.A. and Nelson, J.A. [eds.] 1993).

In her book *Beyond Self-Interest,* Jane J. Mansbridge offers an alternative theory of choice that is inspired by feminine values. She differentiates among three forms of motivation—duty, self-interest, and love. Starting with her own case, she writes the following:

> I have a duty to care for my child, and I am happy by his happiness, and I get a simple sensual pleasure from snuggling close to him as I read him a book. I have a principled commitment to work for women's liberation, and I empathize with women, and I find a way to use some of my work for women as background to a book that advances my academic career. Duty, love (or empathy), and self-interest are intermingled in my actions in a way I can rarely sort out (Mansbridge, J.J. 1990: p. 134).

The separation of non self-interested motives such as love and duty has support from a variety of scholars. Amartya Sen labeled this pair of motives as sympathy and commitment (Sen, A. 1977). Jon Elster differentiates between altruism on the one hand and norms on the other hand (Elster, J. 1989). Christopher Jencks uses the terms empathy and morality (Jencks, C. 1990). In their experimental study on cooperation, Robyn M. Dawes, Alphons J. C. van de Kragt, and John M. Orbell refer to we-feeling and conscience in a similar way (Dawes, R.M. et al. 1990).

More interestingly, Mansbridge's view on the complex motivations of human behavior resembles David Hume's, tripartite scheme of interest-driven, affection-driven, and principle-driven behavior. Several things should be said about this three-part scheme:

> First, according to Hume, actions based on interest can be very dangerous. (...) Second, he assumes, that a person's motives are always mixed. Interests, passions, and norms conspire together to shape every human action. Nevertheless, sometimes one motive predominates and sometimes others. We can therefore speak meaningfully of largely principle-driven, largely interest-driven, and largely affection-driven behavior. (...) Hume does not view self-interest as the hard rock on which all social life is built. He clarifies the nature of self-interested and rational behavior by contrasting it with disinterested and irrational behavior (Holmes, S. 1990: p. 273 and p. 275).

Mansbridge favors the coincidence of duty and love with self-interest. She says that both forms of non self-interested motives (empathic feelings and moral commitments) are embedded in a social context, which makes them susceptible to being undermined by self-interested behavior on the part of others. Arrangements are required that generate some self-interested return to non self-interested behavior to create an "ecological niche" for sustaining such behavior. Arrangements that make non self-interested behavior less costly, in self-interested terms, increase the degree to which individuals feel that they can afford to indulge their feelings of empathy and their moral commitments (Mansbridge, J.J. 1990: pp. 136-137).

3.10 Summary

The rational choice model has been widely used in economics, political science and other social sciences as a basic model of human choice behavior. The model states that in order to be considered rational, the agent should maximize her or his utility function.

The rational choice model does not presuppose anything about the preferences people have. They may have self-centered preferences, altruistic preferences or even sadomasochistic preferences. The rational choice model represents a formal theory that says nothing about what people prefer or should prefer. This model can be called the weak form of rationality.

In both economics and political science we can find a much stronger version of rationality, where the assumptions of self-interest and perfect knowledge are added to the weak form of rationality. Hence we get the Homo Oeconomicus model according to which individuals are rational, exclusively self-interested and have perfect knowledge about the consequences of their choices. The Homo Oeconomicus model does have substantive assumptions about what people want and the manner in which they want it. This model can be referred to as the strong form of rationality.

Herbert A. Simon argues that the rational choice model has very strong claims on human beings. Real world people have poor cognitive capacity and the information available to them is rather limited in most cases. Agents in the real world usually make "satisficing" decisions; that is, they most often choose the first available alternative that is "good enough" for them.

Experimental results indicate that people are myopic in their decisions, may lack skill in predicting their future tastes, and can be led to erroneous choices by fallible memory and the incorrect evaluation of past experiences.

The accuracy of people's hedonic predictions is generally quite poor. Experimental studies suggest that people may have little ability to forecast changes in their hedonic responses to stimuli. Psychological experiments also show that retrospective evaluations should be viewed with greater distrust than introspective reports of current experience. Since individuals use their evaluative memories to guide their choices among future outcomes, deceptive retrospective evaluations may lead to erroneous choices.

Behavioral decision researchers have conducted a number of experiments demonstrating that people systematically violate the axioms of the expected utility theory. The most famous cases are the Allais paradox, the Ellsberg's problem, the preference-reversal effect and the framing effect. These violations of the rational choice model seem to be so fundamental that no hybrid, nearly rational model can possibly capture this type of behavior.

Amartya Sen argues that if real people behaved in the way that is required of them by the rational choice model, then they would act like "rational fools." Sen uses the term "correspondence rationality" to describe the correspondence of choice with the aims and values of the agent. Rational behavior must demand some consistency, but consistency itself can hardly be adequate to ensure the rationality of choice. Internal consistency is not a guarantee of a person's rationality. Rationality as self-interest maximization has additional problems. According to Sen universal selfishness as an actuality may well be false, but universal selfishness as a requirement of rationality is patently absurd. People have complex motivations, both selfish and selfless, in their economic affairs.

Robert Frank developed a model that emphasizes the role of the emotions in making choices. He demonstrates that passions often serve our interest very well indeed because we face important problems that are simply unsolvable by rational action. Material incentives are by no means the only force that governs behavior. Human behavior is directly guided by a complex psychological reward mechanism.

Frank's conclusion is that persons directly motivated to pursue their self-interest are often doomed to fail for exactly that reason. Problems can often be solved by persons who have abandoned the quest for maximal material advantage. The emotions that lead people to behave in irrational ways can indirectly lead to greater material well-being.

Jon Elster contrasts rational action with norm-guided behavior. Rational action is outcome oriented while social norms are not outcome-oriented devices. The basic question is centered around the interaction between social norms and self-interested motivations. People's actions are determined by self-interest and by the norms to which they subscribe. Norms are partly shaped by self-interest because people often adhere to the norms that favor them. However, norms are not fully reducible to self-interest.

Communitarian thinkers forcefully criticize the liberal conception of the self that is at the heart of the rational choice model. Charles Taylor criticizes the liberal conception of the self as being basically an atomistic conception of the person and human agency, focusing exclusively on will and freedom of choice. He defends a relational, intersubjective conception of the self that stresses the social, cultural, historical and linguistic constitution of personal identity.

Michael Sandel stresses the constitutive role of community in the formation of personal identity. He highlights the cognitive dimensions of reflection and deliberation for an adequate view of human agency. Alistair MacIntyre defends a teleological and contextualist view of human agency. According to him, moral conduct is characterized by the exercise of virtues aimed at realization of the good. No agent can properly locate, interpret, and evaluate her or his actions except by participating in a moral tradition or moral community.

Amitai Etzioni developed the I & We paradigm, in which two irreducible sources of valuations play a role, namely pleasure and morality. The relationship between pleasure and morality is that while both affect choice, they also affect one another. However, each factor is only partially shaped by the other; that is, each factor has considerable autonomy.

Etzioni breaks with the rationalist framework of choice. He states that the choices of individuals are governed by normative commitments and affective involvements. The majority of choices people make are based on normative-affective considerations. The limited zones in which logical-empirical considerations are paramount are themselves defined by normative-affective factors that legitimate and motivate such decision making.

The rational choice model can also be criticized from an environmental point of view. It is very questionable that the sustainability of natural systems can be assured on the basis of self-interested individual choices. Since humans are biosocial beings, they have emotions directly associated with the environment and engage themselves in environmental values. These values and emotions are expressed in their preferences and moral commitments.

The feminist literature often criticizes the rational choice theory for presupposing an androcentric, male-biased conception of the human person, the so-called separative self.

Jane J. Mansbridge offers an alternative theory of choice that is inspired by feminine values. She differentiates among three forms of motivation, namely duty, self-interest, and love. Mansbridge's view on the complex motivations of human behavior resembles David Hume's tripartite scheme of interest-driven, affection-driven, and principle-driven behavior. Mansbridge favors the coincidence of duty and love with self-interest.

4. Norms, Goals, and Stakeholders

In this chapter the basic features of complex choice situations will be analyzed.

In Section 4.1 choice is considered as a special form of problem solving. Complex choice situations present ill-structured problems where the solution is far from evident.

Ethical norms appear in complex choice situations. They represent duties for the decision maker. Also, the affected parties (stakeholders) may be identified and perceived by the decision maker (Sections 4.2 and 4.3).

In Section 4.4 it is demonstrated that goals and decision alternatives evolve simultaneously. Both of them are highly influenced by the normative-affective factors of the choice situations.

4.1 Choice as Problem Solving

Choice can best be seen as problem solving (Ackoff, R.L. 1974; Simon, H.A. et al. 1992). The agent happens to be in a situation that is "problematic" for one reason or another. He or she experiences some tension between the perceived state of affairs and the desired state of affairs (Bartee, E.M. 1973).

Complex choice situations present ill-structured problems. A problem is ill-structured if it is not well-structured, which means that at least one of the following criteria does not hold (Simon, H.A. 1977):

(i) There is an unambiguous criterion against which the proposed solutions of the problem can be checked.

(ii) All stages of the problem-solving process can be accurately represented by a model.

(iii) Relevant information is available concerning the problem and its solution.
(iv) There exists a computational method that can solve the problem effectively.

In complex choice situations, usually one or more of the criteria (i),...,(iv) does not hold. Russell L. Ackoff introduces the term "mess" to describe ill-structured problem situations (Ackoff, R.L. 1974).

The decision maker may use some heuristics to structure the mess she or he faces. In behavioral decision research, this process is called framing the decision. The decision maker sets his or her aspirations in the context of the decision. However, the aspirations of the decision maker are joined by normative-affective factors, namely ethical norms that apply in the given situation and perceived other parties that are affected by the outcome of the choice.

4.2 Ethical Norms

In complex choice situations, ethical norms appear since the choice has wide-ranging consequences and other parties are also affected by the outcome of choice. Ethical norms represent duties for the decision maker.

Duties can be classified on different grounds (O'Neill, O. 1992: pp. 274-278).

Duties may or may not have corresponding rights. Duties that have corresponding rights are called perfect duties while duties that do not have such corresponding rights are called imperfect duties. One can think of perfect duties as presenting stronger claims than imperfect duties because other agents can claim the performance of those duties by the decision maker. However, imperfect duties might present strong motivation, too, if they are deeply rooted in the value system of the decision maker.

A distinction can also be made between special duties and universal duties. Special duties are those, which are incumbent on specified agents to provide to others with whom there is some well-defined relationship. This does not hold in the case of universal duties, which are everyone's obligation. For example, particular employers may have special duties to their employees who, in turn, have special rights to their employers' performance of those duties. These are perfect special duties.

There are imperfect special duties, too. For example, parents may think that they ought to provide not only basic care but also vacations for their children. However, this does not imply that children have a right to a vacation.

Universal duties may also be either perfect or imperfect. Perfect universal duties, those duties whose performance everyone can claim as a right, are the responsibility of all to all. The counterparts of liberty rights are perfect universal duties; namely, not to interfere with our fellow beings. Imperfect universal duties are incumbent on all but have no corresponding rights. For example, many of our duties to natural beings and to future generations fall into this category since natural beings and future generations do not have rights in the strict sense of the word.

Duties are also characterized as strict (or narrow) and wide (or broad). These terms are used to contrast duties whose performance is precisely defined with duties that leave more to the agent's interpretation. For example, a wide duty of fairness does not tell us what to do with any precision, but it is nonetheless a strict duty to signal an alarm when the enemy attack becomes obvious.

Certain sets of ethical norms are valid only in one moral tradition or within the boundaries of a particular moral community. Even human rights and their corresponding duties are not completely accepted in every country and culture. Incompatibility between the moral tradition or the moral community of the decision maker and that of the affected parties may lead to conflicts that are difficult-to-resolve. Some ethical algorithms have already been proposed to deal with such problems in multinational business organizations (Donaldson, T. 1982).

4.3 Who Are the Stakeholders?

The term "stakeholder" has been widely used in business and public administration to refer to parties that are affected by the functioning of an organization.

Edward R. Freeman summarizes the history of the stakeholder concept as follows (Freeman, R.E. 1984: pp. 31-51): The term "stakeholder" was introduced by the Stanford Research Institute in 1963 as a generalization of the notion of "stockholder." The stakeholder concept was originally defined as "those groups without whose support the organization would cease to exist." In the 1970s systems theorists, especially Russell L. Ackoff and C. West Churchman, "rediscovered" stakeholder analyses. Ackoff argued that many societal problems could be solved by redesigning fundamental institutions with the support and interaction of the stakeholders in the system (Ackoff, R. L. 1974). During the 1980s and 1990s, the stakeholder approach won considerable acceptance in organization theory, in the corporate social responsibility literature, and also in strategic management.

The standard definition of the concept can be stated as follows: A "stakeholder in an organization is (by definition) any group or individual who can affect or is affected by the achievement of the organization's objectives" (Freeman, E.R. 1984: p. 46).

In the context of moral responsibility, some modification of the stakeholder concept is required. I propose a generalization and, at the same time, an ethical restriction of the notion (Zsolnai, L. 1996). According to the new definition, stakeholders are those beings who are affected by the choice of the decision maker. This definition provides an ethical restriction on the original notion since those parties who can affect the choice but are not affected by it are excluded from classification as stakeholders. Those parties are kibitzers, not stakeholders.

This conceptualization meets the theoretical demand presented by Kenneth E. Goodpaster. All stakeholders are morally considerable, and only those parties that are morally considerable are stakeholders (Goodpaster, K. E. 1991). However, my definition is also a generalization of the original notion since it permits the consideration of beings other than human individuals and groups; namely, biological creatures, ecosystems, and even the Earth as a whole. Similarly, stakeholders are not necessarily actually existing beings. They can be future beings as well.

In contemporary biology, biological creatures are seen as autopoietic systems. "Autopoiesis" means self-making. Chilean biologists Humberto Maturana and Francesco Varella are pioneers in this field. Sometimes their works in the subject are referred as the Santiago theory. According to Maturana and Varella, cognition is an inherent characteristic of all forms of life. A living organism brings forth its world by making distinctions. Cognition results from a pattern of distinctions, and distinctions are perceptions of difference. The Santiago theory describes autonomy of the living organism regarding its response to the environment in the terms of structural coupling and non-linear behavior (Capra, F. 1996: pp. 304-306).

Ecosystems are coexisting populations of plants, animals, and microorganisms in close interaction with sunlight, air, water, and soil. Bioregions such as, for example, the San Francisco Bay, the Danube

River, Amazonia or Siberia can be considered large-scale ecosystems. Ecosystems are supra-individual entities in the sense that their key players are not individual biological creatures but populations. The coexistence of populations is regulated in ecosystems; some populations multiply and flourish while others migrate or become extinct. The long-term dynamic of ecosystems is called succession, which means having a directional change in the structure, form and function of coexisting populations over time. They develop new emphases, as well as different bases and forms. During the succession process, the total biomass production progressively increases; the decomposer elements become larger and more important, and the diversity of species and complexity of their balance grow. In early developmental stages the biomass production exceeds the biomass consumption: There are some niches for new populations. When biomass production and biomass consumption become nearly equal, then ecosystems reach their mature, climax state (Putman, RJ. & Wraten, S.D. 1984).

Now let us turn to the Earth as a whole. James Lovelock shows through his Gaia theory that the Earth is not a passive substratum of life but has itself been playing an active role in conditioning and sustaining life (Lovelock, J. 1979).

A simple thought experiment designed by Lovelock illustrates this point. Let Daisyworld be a planet like the Earth. Over billions of years its sun gets warmer. Daisyworld has nothing but soil and two species of daisy, black and white, competing with each other. Early on, when the sun is young and cool, only the black daisies flourish because they absorb more of the sun's warmth than white daisies do. Their competitive advantage ensures that they spread over the planet. That makes the planet dark, more absorbent of sunlight, and thus warmer. As time goes on, the white daisies, capable of reflecting away more of the sunlight and thus keeping cool, gain the upper hand. The warming effect of black daisies and the cooling effect of white daisies complement each other and the daisies keep the planet at the temperature most suited to them. According to the Gaia theory, the Earth should be viewed as a giant network of all the terrestrial and aquatic ecosystems. The Earth does have systemic patterns and global mechanisms above and beyond any particular ecosystem (Margulis, L. 1998).

Future generations do not yet exist but we have obligations to them. Edith Brown Weiss advances three basic principles concerning future generations (Brown Weis, E. 1989: p. 38).

First, each generation should be required to conserve the diversity of the natural and cultural resource base, so that it does not unduly restrict the options available to future generations in solving their problems. Second, each generation should be required to maintain the quality of the planet so that it is passed on in no worse condition than the present generation received it. Third, each generation should provide access to the legacy from past generations to future generations. These basic principles can be satisfied if we consider every generation as equal and do not presuppose anything about the value preferences of future generations.

Complex choice situations might involve a variety of stakeholders such as existing people and their organizations, the natural environment and even future generations (Figure 3). With some of these stakeholders, the decision maker has contractual responsibility relationships (shareholders, employees, customers and suppliers, for example), while with other stakeholders she or he has natural responsibility relationships (the local community, natural ecosystems, future human beings).

FIGURE 3
Stakeholders in Complex Choice Situations

4.4 Co-Evolving Goals and Alternatives

The classical theory of teleological behavior goes back to Aristotle. It is based on the well-know end-means scheme (Hartman, N. 1966). According to the teleological view of human agency people have well-defined ends and select courses of action as means to attain those ends on logical-empirical bases (Figure 4).

FIGURE 4
The End-Means Scheme

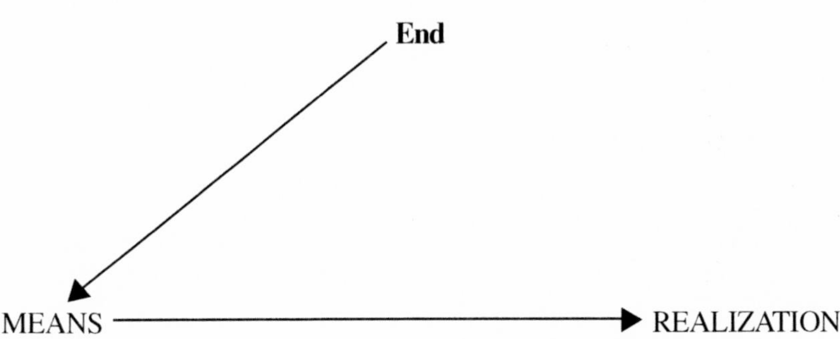

However, every component of this description of human choice behavior can be challenged. Amitai Etzioni points out that logical-empirical factors play only a minor role in human decision making. Normative-affective factors shape decision making to a significant extent:

> Normative-affective factors influence the selection of means by *excluding* the role of logical-empirical considerations in many areas (i.e. choice is made exclusively on normative-affective grounds); in other areas—by *infusing* the deliberation in such a way that logical-empirical considerations play a relatively minor or secondary role to normative-affective factors; and in still others—define the areas in which choices may be made largely or wholly on logical-empirical grounds, areas (...) as normative-affective *indifference zones* (Etzioni, A. 1992: p. 92).

Complex choice situations typically represent the case of infusion in Etzioni's terminology. The applying ethical norms, the aspirations of the decision maker, and the perceived stakeholders together form the normative-affective bases that serve in searching for goals and alternatives.

Goals and alternatives are not independent from each other; rather, they co-evolve. The generated courses of action often influence the goals that they serve to attain. Stanford organizational theorist James G. March and his colleagues developed the so-called garbage can model, according to which goals are usually selected after the decision maker has found feasible alternatives in the choice situation (Cohen, M.D.; March, J.G. and Olsen, J.P. 1978).

The process of choice formation is depicted by Figure 5.

FIGURE 5
The Process of Choice Formation

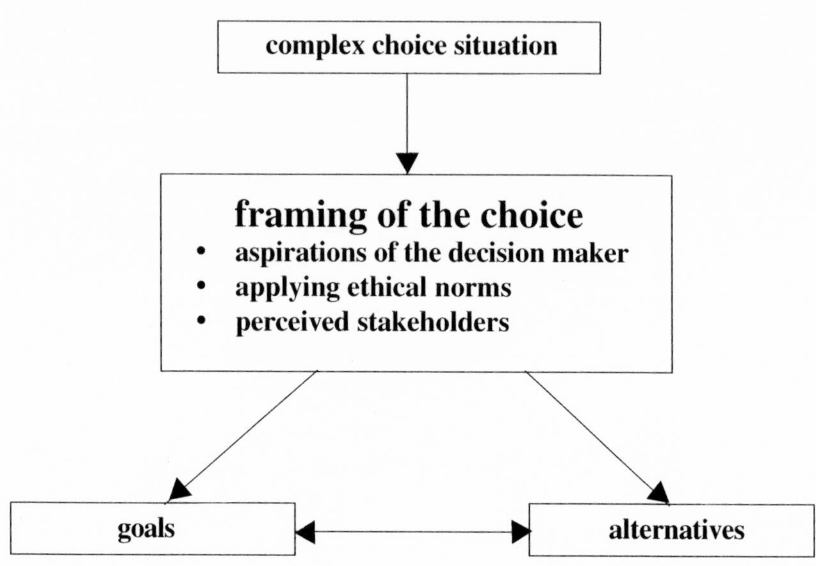

The choice formation is usually an interactive process. The original frame can be restructured in light of the goals and alternatives. The re-fraining of the choice basically depends on the attractiveness of prospects and the time limits of the decision maker.

4.5 Summary

Choice can best be seen as problem solving. The agent happens to be in a situation that is "problematic" for one reason or another. She or he experiences some tension between the perceived state of affairs and the desired state of affairs.

Complex choice situations present ill-structured problems. The decision maker may use some heuristics to structure the "mess" encountered and set aspirations in the context of the decision. However, other normative-affective factors emerge; namely, ethical norms that apply in the given situation and perceived other beings that may be affected by the outcome of the choice.

Ethical norms represent duties for the decision maker. Duties may or may not have corresponding rights. Duties that have corresponding rights are called perfect duties, while duties that do not have such corresponding rights are called imperfect duties. Another important distinction is that between special duties and universal duties. Special duties are obligations of specified agents to others with whom they have some well-defined relationship. This does not hold in the case of universal duties that are incumbent upon everyone to fulfill. Duties are further defined by the terms "strict" (or narrow) and "wide" (or broad). These terms are used to contrast duties whose performance is precisely defined with duties that leave more to the agent's interpretation.

Certain sets of ethical norms are valid only in one moral tradition or within the boundaries of a particular moral community. Incompatibility between the moral tradition or the moral community of the decision maker and that of the affected parties may lead to difficult-to-resolve conflicts.

The term "stakeholder" refers to beings that are affected by the functioning of a business or public organization. All stakeholders are morally considerable, and only those parties that are stakeholders are morally considerable. The definition permits the consideration of parties other than human individuals and groups, namely biological creatures, ecosystems, and even the Earth as a whole. Similarly, stakeholders do not necessarily presently exist beings but can be future beings as well.

Complex choice situations may involve a variety of stakeholders. With some of these stakeholders, the decision maker has contractual-responsibility relationships (shareholders, employees, customers, suppliers) while with other stakeholders she or he has natural-responsibility relationships (the local community, natural ecosystems, future human beings).

The classical theory of teleological behavior is based on the end-means scheme. According to this view human agents have pre-fixed, well-defined ends and select courses of action as means to attain those ends on logical-empirical bases. In real world choice situations, logical-empirical factors play only a minor role in human decision making.

Normative-affective factors shape decision making to a significant extent. In complex choice situations the applying ethical norms, the aspirations of the decision maker, and the perceived stakeholders together form the normative-affective bases that serve in searching for goals and alternatives.

Goals and alternatives are not independent from each other but rather co-evolve. The generated courses of action often influence the goals that they serve to attain. The choice formation is usually an interactive process. The original frame can be restructured in light of the goals and alternatives. The refraining of the choice basically depends on the attractiveness of prospects and the time limits of the decision maker.

5. Responsibility and the Diversity of Choices

In this chapter the model of moral responsibility developed by Kenneth E. Goodpaster will be analyzed. The model identifies rationality and respect for others as two basic components of moral responsibility (Section 5.1).

In Section 5.2 Goodpaster's model is developed further. Responsibility is defined as a synthesis of deontological considerations, rationality in goal-achievement, and respect for the stakeholders.

In Section 5.3 a typology of choice is presented, which differentiate among positive, negative and mixed choices people can make.

5.1 Rationality and Respect

In an economic context, business ethicist Kenneth E. Goodpaster presented the most advanced model of moral responsibility (Goodpaster, K.E. & Matthews, J.B. 1982, Goodpaster, K.E. 1983). Following his philosophy master, William K. Frankena, Goodpaster proposes an understanding of moral responsibility that combines two basic components, namely rationality and respect.

Rationality involves the following attributes:

(i) lack of impulsiveness;
(ii) care in mapping out alternatives and consequences;
(iii) clarity about goals and purposes;
(iv) attention to details of implementation.

Rationality described by attributes (i),...,(iv) radically differs from the rationality postulate of standard economics analyzed in Section 3.1. The rationality concept used here is process oriented and does not require maximizing anything. Max Weber's concept of "zveckrationalitat" and Herbert Simon's, notion of procedural rationality are closely related to it (Weber, M. 1921-1922; Simon, H.A. 1976, 1978).

In Goodpaster's view respect is the other component of moral responsibility:

> The moral point of view also includes a special awareness of and concern for the effects of one's decisions and policies on others, special in the sense that it goes beyond the kind of awareness and concern that would ordinarily be part of rationality, that is, beyond seeing others merely as instrumental to accomplishing one's own purposes. (...) This is respect for the lives of others and involves taking their needs and interests seriously, not simply as resources in one's own decision making but as limiting conditions, which change the very definition of one's habitat from a self-centered to a shared environment (Goodpaster, K.E. & Matthews, J.B. 1982: p. 134).

Respect described in this way has a basic similarity to the altruistic behavior that is widely discussed in economics. Italian economist, Stefano Zamagni, edited a huge volume on the *Economics of Altruism* that contains dozens of papers highlighting the phenomenon (Zamagni, S. (ed.) 1995).

Zamagni offers a clear conceptualization of altruistic behavior. He defines individuals as altruistic "when they feel and act as if the welfare of others were an end in itself; that is, as something of relevance independently of its effects on their own well-being." If your concern for the welfare of others is merely instrumental for promoting your own longer-term ends and ceases once these ends can more easily be pursued in some other way, you are an enlightened self-interested person, not a genuine altruist. Zamagni delineates the sufficient conditions of altruistic behavior as follows: A beneficial behavior actuated either by altruistic reasons only or by a mixture of altruistic and nonaltruistic reasons when the former, in the absence of the latter, would have been sufficient to generate the beneficial behavior (Zamagni, S. 1995: p. xvi).

To repeat, in Goodpaster's model moral responsibility is a combination of rationality and respect in the decision-making context. He writes the following:

> Rationality involves the pursuit of one's projects and purposes with careful attention to ends and means, alternatives and consequences, risks and opportunities. Respect involves consideration of the perspectives of other persons in the pursuit of one's rational projects and purposes. In the words of Kant, respect implies treating others, especially affected parties, as *ends* and not mere means.

It implies a self-imposed constraint on rationality born of a realization that the worth of our projects and purposes resides in the same humanity shared by those who are likely to be affected by them. Taking the "moral point of view" therefore, has both self-directed component (rationality) and other-directed component (respect). These, at least, provide us with an understanding of the spirit that underlines the concept of moral responsibility (Goodpaster, K.E. 1983: p. 7.).

5.2 Deontology

The model of moral responsibility proposed by Goodpaster is basically, but not exclusively, a consequentialist model of choice. This may require some explanation.

The term "consequentialism" was introduced by G.E.M. Anscombe in her article "Modern Moral Philosophy" in the late 1950s. It primarily refers to moral views or theories that base the evaluations of acts solely on the consequences of the acts. (Anscombe, G.E.M. 1958). From the works of Jeremy Bentham, Henry Sidgwick, and George E. Moore, utilitarianism was developed. It represents a special form of consequentialism. Their claim is that the Tightness or obligatoriness of an act depends on whether its consequences are at least as good as or better than those of any alternative act available to the agent, providing that consequences are measured in the terms of happiness, pleasure, well-being, utility, or some combination of these (Slote, M. 1992: p. 211). Nevertheless, consequentialism is a much broader category than utilitarianism, and there are consequentialist systems that are not utilitarian at all (Sen, A.K. & Williams, B. [eds.] 1982).

Consequentialist models can be criticized from consequentialist as well as nonconsequentialist perspectives.

In complex choice situations specific phenomena can emerge that make the consequentialist account of an act very difficult, if not impossible, to accept. The most important of these phenomena are marginal contributions, uncertain consequences, and distant or dispersed effects.

There are cases where the agent's choice produces only marginally negative consequences, but where at the same time the cumulative or aggregate effect of this kind of behavior is detrimental. Ecologist Garret Hardin's famous "tragedy of the commons" model describes such situations (Hardin, G. 1968). If some consequences of an act are rather uncertain, then the decision makers tend to neglect them in their consequentialist considerations. This may lead to inadequate accounting. Similarly, if the consequences of an act are distant or dispersed in space and time, then the decision makers discount them at a positive (and sometimes very high) rate. Hence consequences beyond the normal space-and-time reference of the decision makers are usually overdiscounted (Meadows, D. et al. 1972).

The phenomena of marginal contributions, uncertain consequences, and distant effects present decision traps from which there is no escape within the consequentialist framework.

Consequentialist models are also criticized from a deontological point of view. The essence of deontology is the notion that an act is morally right when it conforms to a relevant principle or duty. Deontology uses as the criterion for judging the morality of an act the moral duty it discharges or disregards, and not the consequences or the ends it aspires to achieve.

Thomas Nagel developed a strong case for deontological reasons entering into complex choice situations. He illustrates the case with well-focused examples. One of these examples is as follows:

> You have an auto accident one winter night on a lonely road. The other passengers are badly injured, the car is out of commission, and the road is deserted, so you run along till you find an isolated house. The house turns out to be occupied by an old woman who is looking after her very small grandchild. There is no phone, but there is a car in the garage, and you ask desperately to borrow it, and explain the situation. She does not believe you. Terrified by your desperation she runs upstairs and locks herself in the bathroom, leaving you alone with the child. You pound ineffectively on the door and search without success for the car keys. Then it occurs to you that she might be persuaded to tell you where they are if you were to twist the child's arm outside the bathroom door. Should you do it? (Nagel, T. 1988: pp. 156-157).

Certainly you should not twist the child's arm; however, this would be only a minor evil compared with your friends' not getting to hospital. You have good deontological reason not to do that. Deontological reasons limit what we may do to others or how we may treat them.

I propose to define respect as altruistic interest in the well-being of the affected parties. In addition, I propose to introduce deontological considerations as a separate component into the model of moral responsibility. This separation of non self-interested motives has considerable support in the economic, psychological and sociological literature that was reported in Section 3.9 (love versus duty).

We can arrive at a robust model of moral responsibility by defining moral responsibility as a practical synthesis of deontological considerations, rationality in goal-achievement, and respect for stakeholders. I propose calling this model of moral responsibility the "3 R model" since responsibility equals reverence plus rationality plus respect. This means that a responsible agent should make choices in a way that displays reverence for the applying ethical norms, promotes the achievement of her or his goals, and shows respect for the affected beings (Figure 6).

FIGURE 6
The 3 R Model of Responsibility

Responsibility = reverence & rationality & respect

5.3 Choices People Can Make

The 3 R model of responsibility provides a framework for analyzing a variety of choices people can make.

Three irreducible aspects of human choice behavior have been identified; namely, the deontological aspect, the rationality aspect, and the stakeholder aspect.

Let $\{\mathbf{A}_i\}$ be the set of available decision alternatives for the agent. Let **D(), G(),** and **S()** be deontological, goal-achievement, and stakeholder value functions, respectively. Hence the agent may have three different evaluations over the decision alternatives. $\mathbf{D}(\mathbf{A}_i)$, $\mathbf{G}(\mathbf{A}_i)$, and $\mathbf{S}(\mathbf{A}_i)$ are decision variables that the agent may use in making her or his choice. Suppose that the agent wants to increase the value of her or his decision variable(s). Hence the following typology emerges:

$$\max \mathbf{D}(\mathbf{A}_i) \tag{5.1}$$

Here the agent increases solely the deontological value of her/his choice. This is the case of deontological choice described by Amitai Etzioni (1988).

$$\max \mathbf{G}(\mathbf{A}_i) \tag{5.2}$$

Here the agent increases solely the goal-achievement value of her/his choice. This is the case of rational choice.

$$\max S(A_i) \tag{5.3}$$

Here the agent increases solely the stakeholder value of her/his choice. This is the case of altruistic choice (Zamagni, S. 1995).

(5.1), (5.2), and (5.3) represent the elementary forms of positive choices people can make in different choice situations. However, there are more complex forms as well.

$$\max [D(A_i), G(A_i)] \tag{5.4}$$

Here the agent increases both the deontological value and the goal-achievement value of her/his choice. This choice might be called the norms-constrained rational choice. In his book Anarchy, State, and Utopia Robert Nozick advances a similar structure for moral agency (Nozick, R. 1974).

$$\max [D(A_i), S(A_i)] \tag{5.5}$$

Here the agent increases both the deontological value and the stakeholder value of her/his choice. This choice might be called the "moral saint" choice since the pursuit of the agent's own goals is not considered at all (Wolf, S. 1982).

$$\max [G(A_i), S(A_i)] \tag{5.6}$$

Here the agent increases both the goal-achievement value and the stakeholder value of her/his choice. This choice might be called the cooperative choice because the agent considers both her/his own interest and the interest of the stakeholders (McCrimmon, K.R. & Messick, D.M. 1976).

$$\max [D(A_i), G(A_i), S(A_i)] \tag{5.7}$$

Here the agent increases the deontological value, the goal-achievement value, and the stakeholder value of her/his choice at the same time. This choice might be called the social-rational choice.

Positive choices defined by (5.1),...,(5.7) can be nicely represented by a lattice structure (Figure 7).

FIGURE 7
The Lattice of Positive Choices

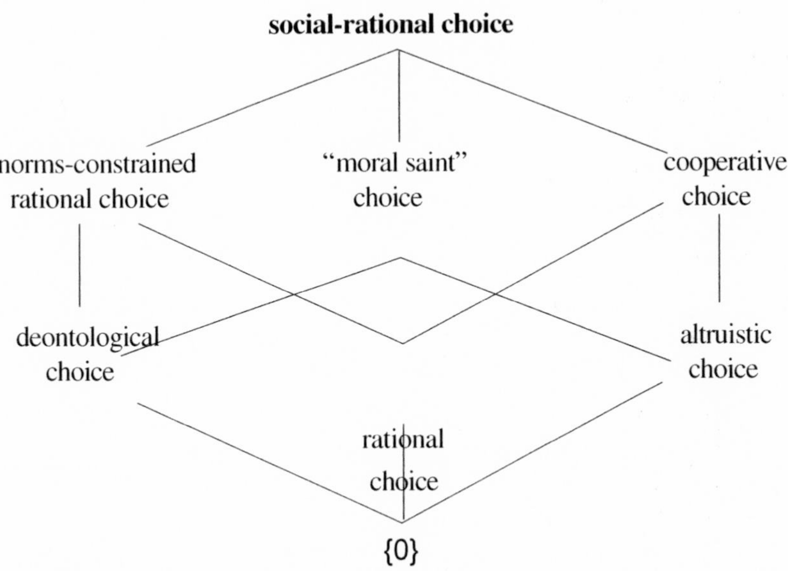

There are negative choices as well. Economist Jack Hirschleifer rightly emphasizes the dark side of the force—to wit, crime, war, and politics. He claims that all aspects of human life are responses to the interaction of two great life-strategy options: on the one hand production and exchange, and on the other hand appropriation and defense against appropriation. We need an equally subtle and structured analysis of the dark side (Hisrschleifer, J. 1994: p. 9).

The agent can make choices that decrease the value of the decision variable(s).

$$\min D(A_i) \qquad (5.8)$$

Here the agent decreases the deontological value of her/his choice. This is the case of antisocial choice. The agent violates the applying norms by her/his choice.

$$\min G(A_i) \qquad (5.9)$$

Here the agent decreases the goal-achievement value of her/his choice. This is the case of irrational choice described by Amartya Sen in Section 3.5.

$$\mathbf{minS(A_i)} \tag{5.10}$$

Here the agent decreases the stakeholder value of her/his choice. This is the case of hostile choice. Studies of envy in economics are related to this type of choice.

$$\mathbf{min\,[D(A_i), G(A_i)]} \tag{5.11}$$

Here the agent decreases both the deontological value and the goal-achievement value of her/his choice. This choice might be called the self-damaging, antisocial choice.

$$\mathbf{min\,[D(A_i), S(A_i)]} \tag{5.12}$$

Here the agent decreases both the deontological value and the stakeholder value of her/his choice. This choice is really the "satanic" choice.

$$\mathbf{min\,[G(A_i), S(A_i)]} \tag{5.13}$$

Here the agent decreases both the goal-achievement value and the stakeholder value of her/his choice. This might be called the destructive choice.

$$\mathbf{min\,[D(A_i), G(A_i), S(A_i)]} \tag{5.14}$$

Here the agent decreases the deontological value, the goal-achievement value, and the stakeholder value of her/his choice at the same time. This is the case of all-negating choice.

Figure 8 presents the lattice of negative choices defined by (5.8),...,(5.14).

FIGURE 8
The Lattice of Negative Choices

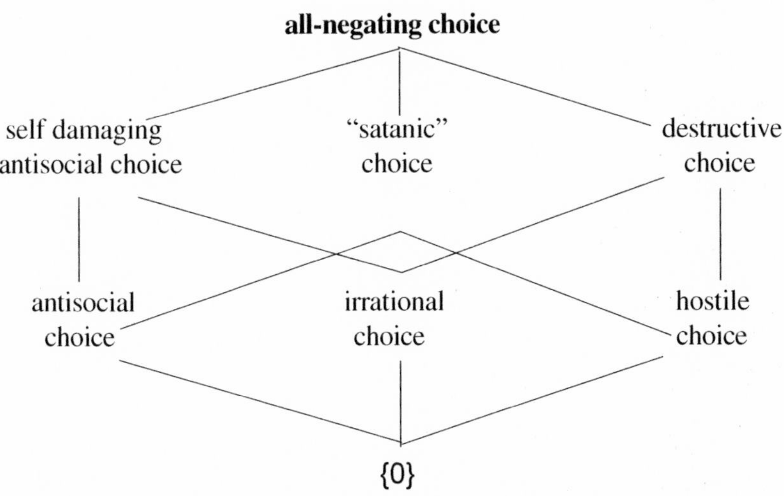

The above-presented typology of choices is not exhaustive at all. There are mixed choices in which different components of positive and negative choices are combined. One of the most important mixed choices is as follows:

$$\max G(A_i) \,\&\, \text{rain}\, [D(A_i), S(A_i)] \qquad (5.15)$$

Here the agent increases the goal-achievement value of her/his choice while at the same time decreasing both the deontological value and the stakeholder value of her/his choice. This is the case of criminal choice, which is a combination of rational choice and "moral evil" choice.

Choice categories (5.1),...,(5.15) are broadly defined. Many of them permit different specifications. Different models can be used in combining the decision variables (lexicographic or horizontal, additive or multiplicative modeling).

5.4 Summary

In an economic context, Kenneth E. Goodpaster has presented the most advanced model of moral responsibility. He proposes an understanding of moral responsibility that combines two basic components, namely rationality and respect.

Rationality involves the following attributes: lack of impulsiveness; care in mapping out alternatives and consequences; clarity about goals and purposes; and attention to details of implementation. This concept of rationality is process oriented and does not require maximizing anything. Respect is the other component of moral responsibility. It means having a special awareness of and concern for the effects of one's decisions and policies on others, beyond seeing others merely as instrumental to accomplishing one's own purposes. Respect described in this way has a basic similarity to the altruistic behavior that is widely discussed in economics.

Consequentialist models can be criticized from consequentialist as well as nonconsequentialist perspectives. In complex choice situations, phenomena can emerge that make the consequentialist account of an act very difficult, if not impossible, to accept. The most important of these phenomena are marginal contributions, uncertain consequences, and distant effects.

There are cases where the agent's choice produces only a marginally negative contribution to the stakeholders, but where at the same time the cumulative and/or aggregate effect of the behavior is detrimental. If some consequences of an act are rather uncertain, decision makers tend to neglect them in their consequentialist considerations. This may lead to inadequate accounting. Similarly, if the consequences of an act are distant in space or time, then the decision makers discount them at a positive (and sometimes very high) rate. Hence consequences beyond the normal space-and-time reference of the decision makers are usually overdiscounted.

Consequentialist models are also criticized from a deontological point of view. The essence of deontology is the notion that an act is morally right when it conforms to a relevant principle or duty. Deontology uses as the criterion for judging the morality of an act the moral duty it discharges or disregards, and not the consequences or the ends it aspires to achieve. There are cases where the decision maker has deontological reason not to do what would result in the best consequences. Deontological reasons limit what we may do to others or how we may treat them.

We can arrive at a robust model of moral responsibility by defining responsibility as a practical synthesis of deontological considerations, rationality in goal-achievement, and respect for the stakeholders. This model of moral responsibility is called the "3 R model" since responsibility equals reverence plus rationality plus respect. A responsible agent makes choices in a way that displays reverence for the applying ethical norms, promotes the achievement of her or his goals, and shows respect for the affected parties.

The 3 R model of responsibility provides a framework for analyzing a variety of choices people can make. It identifies irreducible aspects of human choice behavior, namely the deontological aspect, the rationality aspect, and the stakeholder aspect.

When the agent increases solely the deontological value of her/his choice, a deontological choice is made. When the agent increases solely the goal-achievement value of her or his choice, a rational choice is made. When the agent increases solely the stakeholder value of a choice, then she or he makes an altruistic choice.

There are more complex forms as well. When the agent increases both the deontological value and the goal-achievement value of her/his choice, it might be called a norms-constrained rational choice. When the agent increases both the deontological value and the stakeholder value of her/his choice, it might be called a "moral saint" choice since the pursuit of the agent's own goals is never considered. When the agent increases both the goal-achievement value and the stakeholder value of the choice it might be called a cooperative choice since the agent considers both her/his own interest and the interest of the stakeholders. Finally, when the agent increases the deontological value, the goal-achievement value, and the stakeholder value at the same time, it might be called a social-rational choice.

The agent may make choices that decrease the value of her/his decision variable(s). When the deontological value of the choice is minimized it becomes an anti-social choice. When the agent minimizes the goal-achievement value of the choice it becomes an irrational choice. When the agent minimizes the stakeholder value of the choice then she or he makes a hostile choice.

There are more complex forms of negative choices as well. When the agent decreases both the deontological value and the goal-achievement value of her/his choice, then the choice might be called a self-damaging, anti-social choice. When the agent decreases both the deontological value and the stakeholder value of her/his choice, then it truly represents a "satanic" choice. When the agent decreases both the goal-achievement value and the stakeholder value of her/his choice then it might be called a destructive choice. Finally, when the agent decreases the deontological value, the goal-achievement value, and the stakeholder value of her/his choice all at the same time, then this becomes an example of an all-negating choice.

There are mixed choices in which different components of positive and negative choices are combined. One of the most important mixed choices is when the agent intends to increase the goal-achievement value of her/his choice while simultaneously wishing to decrease both the deontological and stakeholder values of the choice. This is the case of a criminal choice, which combines the rational choice with the satanic choice.

6. The Psychology of Choice

In this chapter some results of decision psychology will be reported that should be given serious consideration in developing a realistic and operationalized model of responsible choice.

In Section 6.1 the prospect theory developed by Daniel Kahneman and Amos Tversky is presented. This theory states the basic empirical features of the value function of decision makers.

In Section 6.2 the so-called matching law, developed by Richard J. Herrnstein, is introduced. According to this law, agents equalize the average reinforcement value of decision alternatives.

Finally, in Section 6.4 Herbert A. Simon's, empirical observations and Reinhard Selten's game experimental results are reported, indicating that people seek to avoid making tradeoffs among different value dimensions in complex choice situations.

6.1 Prospect Theory

The prospect theory was developed by psychologists Daniel Kahneman and Amos Tversky as a new theory of decision under risk, since the expected utility theory is basically untenable from a descriptive point of view (Kahneman, D. and Tversky, A. 1979).

Prospect theory is based on a series of carefully designed experiments, some of which were already reported in Section 3.4.

The essential assumption of the prospect theory is that carriers of value for decision makers are not final states but changes in their wealth or welfare:

> This assumption is compatible with basic principles of perception and judgment. Our perceptual apparatus is attuned to the evaluation of changes or differences rather than to the evaluation of absolute magnitudes. When we respond to attributes such as brightness, loudness, or temperature, the past and present context of experience defines an adaptation level, or reference point, and stimuli are perceived in relation to this reference point. Thus, an object at a given temperature may be experienced as hot or cold to the touch depending on the temperature to which one has adapted. The same principle applies to non-sensory attributes such as health, prestige, and wealth. The same level of wealth, for example, may imply abject poverty for one person and great riches for another—depending on their current assets (Kahneman, D. and Tversky, A. 1979: p. 277).

Kahneman and Tversky state that value is a function of two arguments: the asset position that serves as reference point, and the magnitude of change (positive or negative) from that reference point. Decision makers "code" decision prospects in terms of gains and losses. The central hypothesis of prospect theory is that the value function of decision makers is concave for gains and convex for losses. This hypothesis is illustrated by the following decision problems (Kahneman, D. and Tversky, A. 1979: p. 278):

Problem (I) Choose between
(A) **25%** chance to win **$6,000**
(B) **25%** chance to win **$4,000** and **25%** chance to win **$2,000**

A total of **82 percent** of the subjects chose prospect **(B)** and only **18 percent** chose prospect **(A)**. Notice that the expected utility is **$1,500** in both cases.

The next problem is the negative version of problem (I).

Problem (II) Choose between
(C) **25%** chance to lose **$6,000**
(D) **25%** chance to lose **$4,000** and **25%** chance to lose **$2,000**

The expected utility is **$1,500** in both cases. However, **70 percent** of the subjects chose prospect **(C)** and only **30 percent** of them chose prospect **(D)**.

These disturbing results nicely correspond to the central hypotheses of prospect theory, since

$$V(\$6{,}000) < V(\$4{,}000) + V(\$2{,}000)$$

and

$$V(-\$6{,}000) < V(-\$4{,}000) + V(-\$2{,}000),$$

where **V( )** is the value function.

A salient characteristic of people's attitudes to changes in welfare is that losses loom larger than gains:

> The aggravation that one experiences in losing a sum of money appears to be greater than the pleasure associated with gaining the same amount. Indeed, most people find symmetric bets of the form **(x, 0.50; -x, 0.50)** distinctively unattractive. Moreover, the aversiveness of symmetrically fair bets generally increases with the size of the stake. That is, if **x > y > 0**, then **(y, 0.50; -y, 0.50)** is preferred to **(x, 0.50; -x, 0.50)** (Kahneman, D. and Tversky, A. 1979: p. 279).

The main statement of prospect theory is that the value function is steeper for losses than for gains. That is

$$V(x) < -V(-x) \tag{6.1}$$

This means that decision makers are more sensitive to losses than to gains.

Other experiments show that the ratio of the slopes in the domains of losses and gains, the so-called loss aversion coefficient, might be estimated as about 2:1 (Tversky, A. and Kahneman, D. 1991, 1992).

That is

$$2V(x) \approx -V(-x) \tag{6.2}$$

To sum up, prospect theory proposes that the decision maker's value function is

(i) generally concave for gains and convex for losses;
(ii) steeper for losses than for gains.

The shape of the value function is displayed in Figure 9.

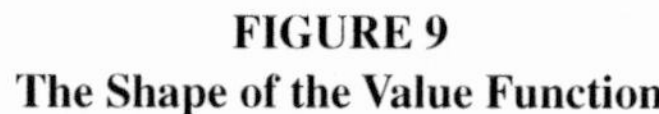

FIGURE 9
The Shape of the Value Function

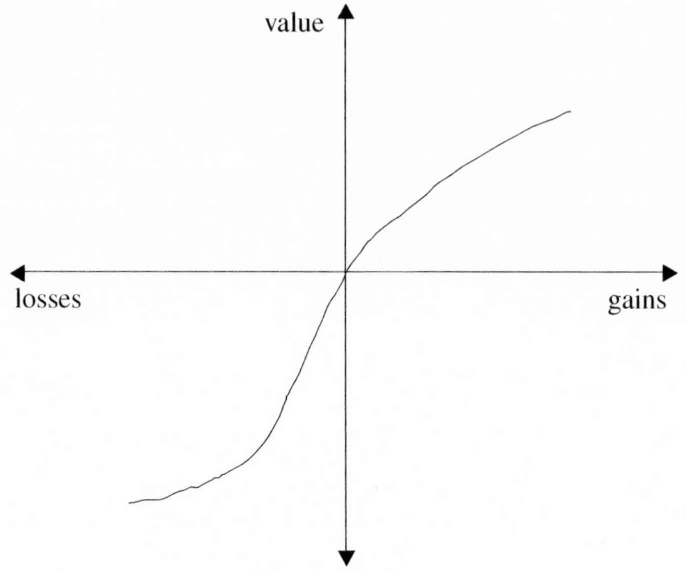

Source: Kahneman, D. & Tversky, A. 1979: p. 279.

Since its birth, the prospect theory has obtained overwhelming empirical evidence that support its main propositions (Thaler, R.H. 1991).

6.2 The "Matching Law"

After decades of experimental work, Harvard psychologist Richard J. Herrnstein formulated his "matching law" (Herrnstein, RJ. 1961,1970, 1993). The matching law states that "at equilibrium, an individual's behavior is distributed over alternatives in the choice set so as to equalize the reinforcement returns per unit of behavior invested, measured in time, effort, or any other dimension of behavior constrained to a finite total" (Herrnstein, RJ. 1993: p. 140).

The salient difference between the matching law and the utility maximization principle is that matching is based on average returns while maximization requires a sensitivity to marginal returns (in utility or reinforcement). Sometimes this does not lead to considerable differences in the outcomes of choice, but in many cases it does.

The following example can serve as an illustration of the point (Herrnstein, RJ. 1993: pp. 141-146). Two commodities are given for a subject in a way that the consumption of the commodities is exhaustive and mutually exclusive. The average utility or reinforcement obtained from each commodity is inversely and linearly related to their consumption. Figure 10 shows the linearly decreasing utility indifference (that is, equal reinforcement) curve that forms a tangent with the "budget constraint." The indifference curve is at a total of 6.9 reinforcement. "O" indicates the point that conforms to the utility maximum while "M" indicates the point that conforms to matching.

FIGURE 10
Matching versus Maximizing

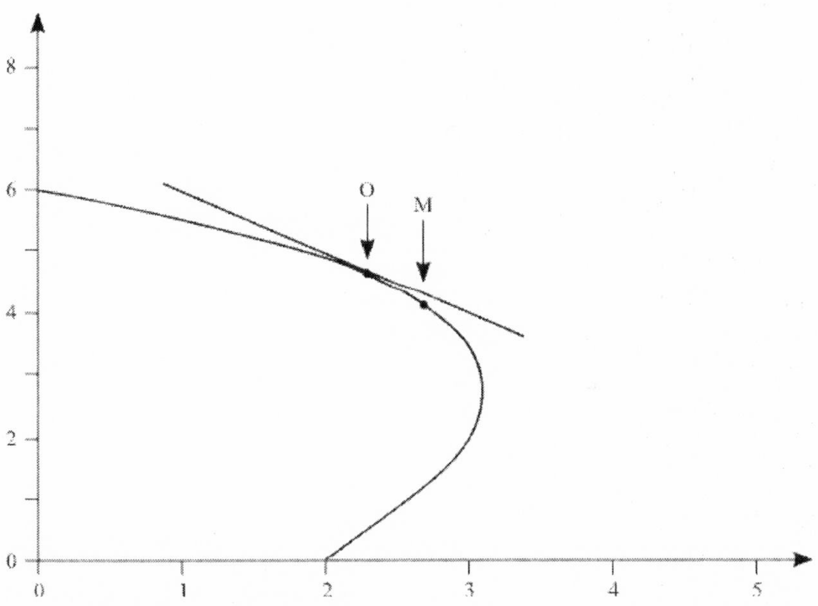

Source: Herrnstein, RJ. 1993: p. 146.

In situations like this, subjects allocate suboptimally because of matching. They equalize average satisfaction or value at some cost in overall gains. In Stevens' *Handbook of Experimental Psychology,* the following is stated about the matching law:

The generality of matching relation has been confirmed by a large number of different experiments. Such studies have shown matching, at least to a first approximation, with different species (pigeons, humans, monkeys, rats), different responses (key-pecking, lever pressing, eye movements, verbal responses), and different reinforcers (food, brain stimulation, money, cocaine, verbal approval). Apparently, the matching relation is a general law of choice (Williams, B.A. 1988).

6.3 Incommensurability

In complex choice situations the decision maker has multiple goals that she or he would like to achieve. In addition, ethical norms apply in the situation and various stakeholders are present. It is quite possible, or even necessary, that these different factors produce incommensurability for the decision maker.

Herbert A. Simon identifies three broad classes of cases where incommensurability is especially likely to intrude (Simon, H.A. 1987: p. 244).

1. Cases of uncertainty, where, for each alternative a bad outcome under one contingency must be balanced against a good outcome under another.
2. Cases of multiperson choice, where one person's gain is another person's loss.
3. Cases of value conflict, where each choice involves gain in one dimension of value and loss along another, very different value dimension.

It has been observed empirically that in circumstances of incommensurability, decision makers seek to avoid making tradeoffs among different value dimensions (Simon, H.A. 1987: p. 244). These observations are confirmed by the game experimental results of the other Nobel Prize laureate economist, Reinhard Selten (Selten, R. 1994: p. 42).

The natural decision-making heuristic in situations of incommensurability is to concentrate initially on improving what appears to be the most critical problem area until some satisfactory level of performance is reached (Simon, H.A. 1976: pp. 272-273).

The so-called reference-point approach of multiple-criteria decision making formalizes this heuristic and provides robust methodologies for the decision maker in the case of incommensurability (Stewart, T.J. 1992: pp. 576-579). In management science, the new idea of "trade-off free" management has emerged (Zeleney, M. 1995).

6.4 Summary

Some results of decision psychology should be seriously examined to arrive at a realistic and operationalized model of ethical decision making.

The prospect theory, developed by Daniel Kahneman and Amos Tversky, is an alternative theory of decision-under-risk. Kahneman and Tversky found that value is a function of two arguments: the asset position that serves as reference point, and the magnitude of change (positive or negative) from that reference point. Decision makers "code" decision prospects in terms of gains and losses. The central hypothesis of prospect theory is that the value function of decision makers is concave for gains and convex for losses. A salient characteristic of people's attitudes to changes in welfare is that losses loom larger than gains. The value function is steeper for losses than for gains since decision makers are more sensitive to losses than to gains.

After decades of experimental work in the laboratory, Harvard psychologist Richard J. Herrnstein formulated his famous "matching law." The salient difference between the matching law and the utility maximization principle is that matching is based on average returns while maximization requires a sensitivity to marginal returns (in utility or reinforcement). Human subjects allocate suboptimally because of matching. They equalize average satisfaction or value at some cost in overall gains.

In complex choice situations, a variety of normative-affective factors may produce incommensurability for the decision maker. It has been observed empirically that in circumstances of incommensurability, decision makers seek to avoid making tradeoffs among different value dimensions. The natural decision-making heuristic in situations of incommensurability is to concentrate initially on improving what appears to be the most critical problem area until it reaches some satisfactory level of performance.

7. Modeling Responsible Decision Making

In this chapter an operationalized model of ethical decision making will be presented.

In Section 7.1 the *basic elements* of complex choice situations are formalized.

In Section 7.2 a deontological value function is defined by which the decision maker can evaluate the decision alternatives from the perspectives of the applying ethical norms.

In Section 7.3 a goal-achievement value function is introduced by which the decision maker can evaluate the decision alternatives in light of the achievement of her/his goals.

In Section 7.4 a stakeholder value function is created by which the decision maker can evaluate the decision alternatives on the basis of their payoffs for the stakeholders.

In Section 7.5 an evaluation matrix is provided that makes it possible for the decision maker to look at the decision alternatives from multiple value perspectives, holding together the deontological, goal-achievement, and stakeholder values of the decision alternatives.

In Section 7.6 the maximin rule is proposed for making a responsible choice. The rule selects the least worst alternative in the decision space of deontological, goal-achievement, and stakeholder values. It is demonstrated that under specific conditions, the responsible decision making model collapses into the rational choice model.

In Section 7.7 a geometric representation of the responsible choice is presented.

In Section 7.8 a verbal description of the procedure of making responsible decisions is provided.

7.1 What is Responsible Decision?

In complex choice situations, the following basic elements can be identified. First, at least two decision alternatives are available for the decision maker; that is, she or he can choose among different courses of action. Second, in the choice situation ethical norms apply that represent duties of the decision maker. Third, the decision maker has goals that she or he wants to achieve in the choice situation. Finally, different stakeholders are present that can be affected by the outcome of the choice.

We can formalize the above-listed elements of complex choice situations as follows:

$$\mathbf{A_1,\ldots,A_i,\ldots,A_m} \qquad \mathbf{(m \geq 2)} \tag{7.1}$$

This means that at least two decision alternatives are available for the decision maker.

$$\mathbf{D_1,\ldots,D_k,\ldots,D_p} \qquad \mathbf{(p \geq 1)} \tag{7.2}$$

This means that at least one ethical norm applies in the choice situation.

$$\mathbf{G_1,\ldots,\ G_j,\ldots G_n} \qquad \mathbf{(n \geq 1)} \tag{7.3}$$

This means that the decision maker has at least one goal that she or he wants to achieve.

$$\mathbf{S_1,\ldots,S_q,\ldots,S_r} \qquad \mathbf{(r \geq 1)} \tag{7.4}$$

This means that at least one stakeholder is present in the choice situation.

Responsible decision making involves finding and implementing the decision alternative that realizes the idea of responsibility in the given context.

In Section 2.3 Hans Jonas' *Imperative of Responsibility*, the essential message of which is the necessity of caring for the beings in the agent's environment, was reviewed. In Section 5.2 a more analytical idea of moral responsibility was developed. Responsibility was defined as a synthesis of reverence for the applying ethical norms, rationality in goal achievement, and respect for the affected parties.

Now we are in the position to pose a crucial question: Which is the appropriate decision rule for making a responsible choice?

$$\mathbf{A}^* = \Omega\ (\mathbf{A}_1,\ldots,\mathbf{A}_i,\ldots,\mathbf{A}_m) \qquad (7.5)$$

where **A*** refers to the selected alternative.

We are searching for the decision rule Ω. that selects the responsible course of action among those courses available to the decision maker.

7.2 Deontological Payoffs

A deontological payoff is defined as the value of a decision alternative seen from the perspective of the applying ethical norms.

The value of decision alternative **Aj** regarding ethical norm $\mathbf{D}_k$ can be calculated by the deontological value function $\mathbf{D}_k()$ as follows:

$$\mathbf{D}_k(\mathbf{Aj}) = \begin{cases} \mathbf{1} & \text{if decision alternative } \mathbf{Aj} \text{ corresponds to ethical norm } \mathbf{D}_k; \\ \mathbf{0} & \text{if decision alternative AJ is neutral regarding ethical norm } \mathbf{D}_k; \\ \mathbf{-2} & \text{if decision alternative } \mathbf{A}_i \text{ violates ethical norm } \mathbf{D}_k. \end{cases} \qquad (7.6)$$

$\mathbf{D}_k(\mathbf{A}_i)$ characteristically shows the payoff of the decision alternative AJ regarding ethical norm $\mathbf{D}_k$.

$\mathbf{D}_k(\ )$ reflects the psychological regularity that the value of the correspondence to a norm is usually much smaller than the value of the violation of the same norm. In other words, $\mathbf{D}_k(\ )$ is a Tversky-Kahneman type of value function since (7.6) satisfies both (6.1) and (6.2).

Figure 11 shows the deontological value function.

FIGURE 11
The Deontological Value Function

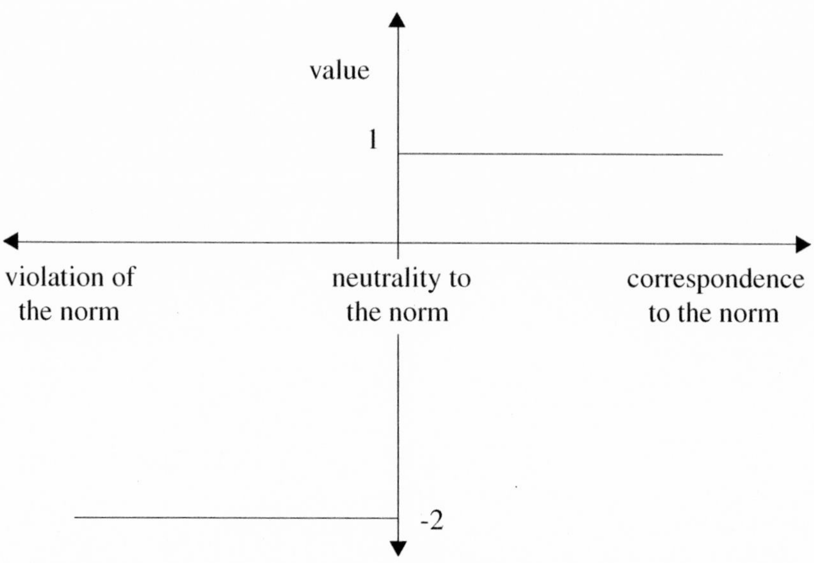

$\mathbf{D_k(A_i)}$ gives a partial evaluation of the decision alternative $\mathbf{A_i}$ because it sees Aj regarding only one ethical norm. An aggregate deontological value function D( ) should be constructed to get an overall picture of how the decision alternative Aj works regarding all the applying ethical norms $\mathbf{D_1,...,D_k,...,D_p}$.

Let $\mathbf{w_1,...,w_k,...,w_p}$ be weights that reflect the relative importance of the ethical norms $\mathbf{D_1,...,D_k,...,D_p}$ in the choice situation.

It is first required that

$$\sum \mathbf{w_k = 1} \qquad \mathbf{(k = l,...,p)} \tag{7.7}$$

After this, the aggregate deontological value of decision alternative j is defined as follows:

$$\mathbf{D(A_i) = \sum w_k D_k(A_i)} \qquad \mathbf{(k = l,...,p)} \tag{7.8}$$

This is a linear averaging model that shows the aggregate deontological payoff of the decision alternative A_i. This formulation is consistent with the matching law introduced in Section 6.2. It is also supported by the work experience of decision analysts who favor the use of additive value functions in their daily decision support work (Stewart, TJ. 1992).

The deontological payoffs of the decision alternatives $\mathbf{A_i,\dots,A_i,\dots,A_m}$ can be represented by a vector as follows:

$$\underline{\mathbf{d}}= [\mathbf{D(A_1),\dots,D(A_k),\dots,D(A_m)}] \tag{7.9}$$

The aggregate deontological payoffs of decision alternatives depend on two things.

(i) Which are the considered ethical norms?
(ii) How are the importance weights assessed?

The desirable properties that should be satisfied by the set of considered ethical norms are as follows:

(i) completeness—all the relevant ethical norms should be included;
(ii) discreteness—double counting should be avoided;
(iii) unambiguity—norms should be clear in their meaning;
(iv) strictness—norms should be defined in narrow rather than broad terms.

(See Keeney, R.L. & Raiffa, H. 1976; Saaty, T.L. 1980; von Winterfeldt, D. & Edwards, W. 1986)

For assessing the weights, any method can be used that produces importance weights measured at least on an interval scale (Stewart, T.J. 1992).

7.3 Goal-Achievement Values

It is natural that the decision maker considers the value of the decision alternatives from the perspective of the achievement of his or her goals. In classical decision theory, this was the only dimension in which courses of action were evaluated and decided upon.

We can define the goal-achievement value function $\mathbf{G_j}(\ )$ as follows:

$$\mathbf{G_j(A_j)} = \begin{cases} \mathbf{1} & \text{if decision alternative } \mathbf{A_i} \text{ is positive for the achievement of goal } \mathbf{G_j}; \\ \mathbf{0} & \text{if decision alternative } A_i \text{ is neutral for the achievement of goal } \mathbf{G_j}; \\ \mathbf{-2} & \text{if decision alternative } \mathbf{A_i} \text{ is negative for the achievement of goal } \mathbf{G_j}. \end{cases} \tag{7-10}$$

$\mathbf{G_j(A_i)}$ characteristically shows the value of decision alternative $\mathbf{A_i}$ regarding the achievement of the decision maker's goal $\mathbf{G_j}$.

$\mathbf{G_j(\,)}$ reflects the psychological regularity that the value of achievement of a certain goal is usually smaller than the value of failure to achieve the same goal. In other words, $\mathbf{G_j(\,)}$ is also Tversky-Kahneman type of value function since (7.10) satisfies both (6.1) and (6.2). Figure 12 shows the goal-achievement value function.

FIGURE 12
Goal-Achievement Value Function

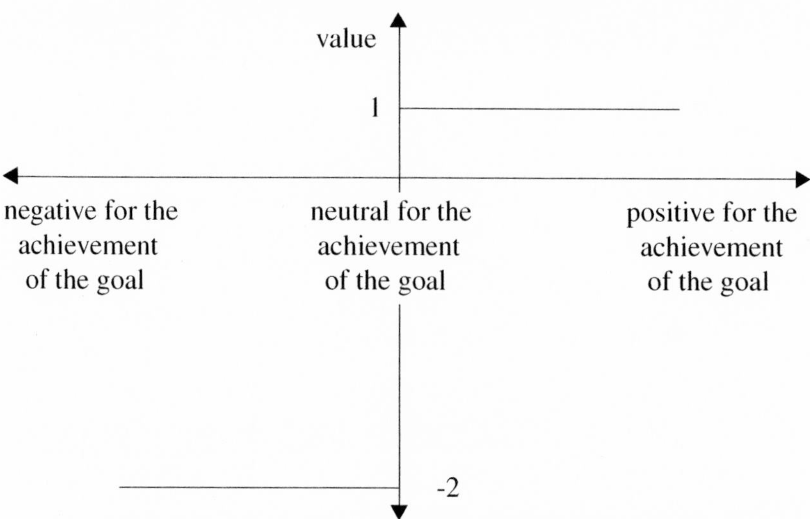

$\mathbf{G_j(A_i)}$ gives a partial evaluation of the decision alternative $\mathbf{A_i}$ because it sees $\mathbf{A_i}$ regarding only one goal. An aggregate goal-achievement value function $\mathbf{G()}$ should be construed to get an overall picture of how the decision alternative $\mathbf{A_i}$ works regarding all the goals to be achieved $\mathbf{G_1,\ldots,G_j,\ldots,G_n}$.

Let $\mathbf{u_1,\ldots,u_j,\ldots,u_n}$ be weights that represent the relative importance of the goals $\mathbf{G_1,\ldots,G_j,\ldots,G_n}$ for the decision maker.

It is required that

$$\sum \mathbf{u_j = 1} \qquad \mathbf{(j = l,\ldots,n)} \tag{7.11}$$

The aggregate goal-achievement value of decision alternative $\mathbf{A_i}$ is defined as follows:

$$G(A_i) = \sum U_j \, G_j(A_i) \qquad (j = 1,\dots,n) \tag{7.12}$$

This is a linear averaging model like (7.10). The reason for choosing this type of model is, mutatis mutandis, the same.

The goal-achievement value of the decision alternatives $A_1,\dots,A_i,\dots,A_m$ can be represented by a vector.

$$\underline{g} = [G(A_1),\dots,G(A_i),\dots,G(A_m)] \tag{7.13}$$

The important question is to what extent the decision maker is free to choose her/his goals and the weights she or he attributes to the chosen goals.

The rational choice theory suggests that the decision maker is completely free to both select her or his goals and weight them. However, the decision maker is embedded in interpersonal relations and the social context, as presented in Section 3.8 (Granovetter, M. 1985, Etzioni, A. 1988). So it is realistic to presuppose that the decision maker sets goals and assigns weights with reference to those communities and organizations of which she or he happens to be a part.

7.4 Payoffs for the Stakeholders

Stakeholders are present in complex choice situations and the decision alternatives render different payoffs for them.

The payoff of decision alternative A_i for the stakeholder S_q can be calculated by stakeholder value function $S_q()$ as follows:

$$S_q(A_i) = \begin{cases} 1 & \text{if decision alternative } A_j \text{ is good for stakeholder } S_q; \\ 0 & \text{if decision alternative } A_i \text{ is neutral for stakeholder } S_q; \\ -2 & \text{if decision alternative } A_i \text{ is bad for stakeholder } S_q. \end{cases} \tag{7-14}$$

$S_q(A_i)$ characteristically shows the value of decision alternative A_i regarding stakeholder S_q.

$S_q(\ )$ reflects the psychological regularity that the value of a positive impact on a stakeholder is usually much smaller than the value of a negative impact of the same magnitude on the same stakeholder. In other words, $S_q(\ )$ is also a Tversky-Kahneman type of value function like (7.6) and (7.10).

Figure 13 shows the stakeholder value function.

FIGURE 13
The Stakeholder Value Function

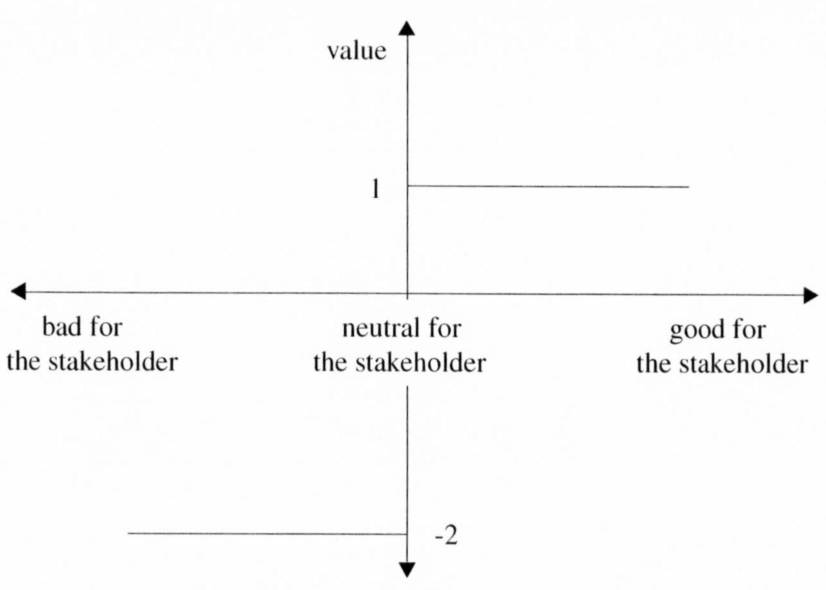

$S_q(A_i)$ gives a partial evaluation of the decision alternative A_i as seen in relation to only one stakeholder S_q. An aggregate stakeholder value function S( ) should be construed to get an overall picture of how the decision alternative A_i works regarding all the stakeholders $S_i,...,S_q,...,S_r$.

Let $v_i,...,v_q,...,v_r$ be weights that reflect the relative importance of stakeholders $S_i,...,S_q,...,S_r$ in the choice situation. It is required that

$$\sum v_q = 1 \quad (q = 1,...,r) \qquad (7.15)$$

Then the aggregate stakeholder value of decision alternative A_i is defined as follows:

$$\mathbf{S(A_i) = \sum v_q\, S_q(A_i) \qquad (q = 1,...,r)} \qquad (7.16)$$

$\mathbf{S_q(A_j)}$ shows the aggregate stakeholder value of decision alternative Aj. The linear-averaging model is used again, but in this case it requires some further explanation.

The linear-averaging model implies that there is a compensatory relationship between one stakeholder's loss and another stakeholder's gain. In reality this is not exactly the case. Stakeholders represent distinct "minds" in the sense Gregory Bateson uses (Bateson, G. 1979). However, this does not mean that for decision-making purposes we cannot produce an aggregate assessment of the gains and losses of different stakeholders. If we use appropriate weights we can get a fair picture, even while using a compensatory model.

The stakeholder payoffs of decision alternatives $\mathbf{A_i,...,A_i,...,A_m}$ can be represented by a vector:

$$\mathbf{S = [S(A_1),...,S(A_i),...,S(A_m)]} \qquad (7.17)$$

The question centers around which parties should be included among the stakeholders in the evaluation of decision alternatives.

Stakeholders usually voice their concerns in some manner to the decision makers (Hirschman, A.0.1977). However, many times affected parties are unable to represent their claims or are incapable of doing so in an effective way. These stakeholders include children, the poor, marginalized or disabled people, the natural environment, and future generations. These stakeholders need advocates who can represent their concerns in a dialogue with the decision maker.

The weighting of the stakeholders introduces difficult questions. Any distribution of weights generates some form of justice or injustice among the stakeholders. I do agree with Michael Walzer that an adequate conception of justice is necessarily plural, that is, multidimensional (Walzer, M. 1983).

I propose using two variables according to which stakeholders can be weighed against one another. One variable is their stake while the other is their size. The greater the stake and the size of a stakeholder, the greater the weight that should be attributed to it. Notice that there is no such thing as zero weighting if at least two parties are present. If one does not attribute weights to the parties, then she or he considers them as being equal. Having no weights means attributing equal weights.

7.5 Evaluation from Multiple Perspectives

Holding (7.9), (7.13), and (7.17) together we can arrive at a multiple evaluation of the decision alternative **A;**

$$\underline{\mathbf{v}} = [\mathbf{D}(\mathbf{A}_i), \mathbf{G}(\mathbf{A}_i), \mathbf{S}(\mathbf{A}_i)] \qquad (7.18)$$

The first component of the vector is the deontological value of the decision alternative; the second component is the goal-achievement value of the decision alternative; while the third component is the stakeholder value of the decision alternative.

Amartya Sen introduced the concept of "goal rights systems," by which he means moral accounting systems where the fulfillment and nonrealization of rights are incorporated in the evaluation of states of affairs (Sen, A. 1982, 1983, 1985).

Sen lists the characteristics of the goal rights systems as follows:

> First, the goal rights systems form a *wide class* rather than representing some unique moral position. There are many sources of difference, for example, what rights to include among the goals, in what form they are to be included, what non-right values (if any) are to be admitted, what weights to use, how should choice of actions be related to the evaluation of outcomes. Second, although rights are included within the evaluation of states of affairs, there could be other things to which the evaluation of states of affairs is sensitive in a goal rights system. The crucial issue is the inclusion *of fulfillment* and *non-fulfillment* of *rights*—rather than the exclusion of non-right considerations—in the evaluation of states of affairs. Third, while *sensitivity* of action-evaluation to consequences is essential for a rights-consequence system, such a system need not be fully consequentialist. Fourth, it may be worth emphasizing that, although a goal rights system incorporates a goal-included view of rights, it does not reject the instrumental relevance of rights either (Sen, A. 1982: p. 199.).

The moral accounting system used in the responsible choice model may be considered a subclass of Sen's goal rights systems. However, there is an important difference. Our accounting system permits and even encourages the incorporation of those ethical norms that do not have corresponding rights, while this is not permitted in the goal rights systems. In this sense the accounting system advanced here represents a broader category than Sen's goal rights systems.

The responsibility calculus advanced here is close to Sen's own ideal about the moral evaluation of acts. He writes in his influential book *On Ethics & Economics:*

To get an overall assessment of the ethical standing of an activity it is necessary not only to look at its own intrinsic value (if any), but also its instrumental role and its consequences on other things.(...) The advantages of consequential reasoning involving interdependence and instrumental accounting, can then be combined not only with intrinsic valuation, but also with position relativity and agent sensitivity of moral assessment (Sen, A. 1987: p. 75 and p. 77.).

Our proposed moral accounting system tries to do this job.

7.6 The Maximin Rule

A complete picture of the choice situation can be provided by a matrix that contains multiple evaluations of all the decision alternatives available for the decision maker.

$$\underline{\mathbf{V}} = \begin{matrix} \mathbf{D(A_1, \ldots\ldots, G(A_1), \ldots.., S(A_1)} \\ \cdot \quad \cdot \quad \cdot \\ \cdot \quad \cdot \quad \cdot \\ \mathbf{D(A_i, \ldots\ldots, G(A_i), \ldots\ldots, S(A_i)} \\ \cdot \quad \cdot \quad \cdot \\ \cdot \quad \cdot \quad \cdot \\ \mathbf{D(A_m), \ldots.., G(A_m), \ldots., S(A_m)} \end{matrix} \qquad (7.19)$$

The *matrix* $\underline{\mathbf{V}}$ may present incommensurability of different kinds for the decision maker as discussed in Section 6.3.

This situation is called unresolved value conflict by Isaac Levi in his treatment of "hard choices" (Levi, 1.1986). Levi's proposal for making a choice under unresolved value conflict is that the decision maker should prioritize the conflicting values and select the best alternative by using a lexicographic decision rule. That is, the decision maker should choose the decision alternative whose performance is the best according to the highest ranked value in the given situation.

In a complex choice situation, the application of the lexicographic rule is rather unattractive and even counterproductive. It reduces the multidimensionality of the choice situation to one dimension. In the end, the decision maker using the lexicographic rule arrives at the choice exclusively through a deontological, rational, or altruistic framework (See Section 5.3). This is not a solution because none of these elementary choice frameworks corresponds well enough to the idea of responsibility discussed in Chapters 2 and 5.

Another possibility is to maintain the complexity of the choice situation and try to find an optimal balance among diverse value dimensions. The maximin rule can do the required job quite well. It implies the maximization of the minimum payoff of decision alternatives. (In Latin it means "maximum minimorum"; that is, the maximum of minimums.)

The maximin rule is intuitively known by chess players. However, it was first described by Austrian logician Ernest Zermello in 1912. The rule was developed further by the Hungarian-American mathematical genius John von Neumann in his ground-breaking *Theory of Games and Economic Behavior* (von Neuman, J. and Morgenstern, O. 1944).

The rule of ethical decision making is stated as follows:

$$\mathbf{A^* = maximin\ [D(A_i), G(A_i), S(A_i)]} \qquad (7.20)$$

Responsible decision making demands the selection of the least worst alternative in the decision space of deontological, goal-achievement, and stakeholder values, in the sense that the minimum value of the selected alternative is greater than the minimum value of any other alternative available to the decision maker in the given situation.

If there are two decision alternatives, A_l and A_2, then the responsible decision making model requires the selection of Al if and only if

$$\mathbf{min\ [D(A_1), G(A_1), S(A_1) > min\ [D(A_2), G(A_2), S(A_2)]} \qquad (7.21)$$

The underlying principle of responsible choice is that the decision maker should find an optimal balance among the applying ethical norms, his or her own goals, and the interest of the stakeholders.

Responsible decision making defined by (7.20) provides a Pareto optimal result in the multidimensional decision space. This means that given the set of decision alternatives, it is not possible to increase their payoff in one value dimension without decreasing their payoff in at least one other value dimension. In this sense the alternative chosen by the maximin rule dominates all the other alternatives.

This may lead to the rehabilitation of the Pareto-principle, whose application in welfare economics is often criticized. In welfare economics a social state is called Pareto optimal or Pareto efficient if and only if no one's utility can be raised without reducing the utility of someone else. When applied in this way the Pareto principle can provide a defense for some social states that are otherwise unacceptable in a moral sense. "A state can be Pareto optimal with some people in extreme misery and others rolling in luxury, so long as the miserable cannot be made better off without cutting into the luxury of the rich. Pareto optimality can, like "Caesar's spirit," come hot from hell (Sen, A. 1987: pp. 31-32).

But if we disconnect the Pareto principle from "welfarism" and apply it in a multidimensional context where values are incommensurable, then it may prove to be a very ethical principle.

The maximin rule can be expressed in another form by using the "Tchebycheff measure." In this case the distance of the actual payoffs from the maximal possible payoffs should be minimized across different value dimensions. This is the "minimax" formulation of the decision rule. Mathematically, both the maximin and minimax formulations perform equally well, but the former is psychologically more realistic than the latter. For this reason I prefer to use the maximin formulation (See Section 6.3).

It is important to demonstrate that the rational choice is a reduced form of responsible decision making. The rule of the rational choice is as follows:

$$\mathbf{A^* = max\ G(A_i)} \qquad (7.22)$$

It is equivalent to (7.20) if there are no applying ethical norms and there are no stakeholders in the choice situation.

If $\mathbf{D_1,...,D_k,...,D_n}$ and $\mathbf{S_1,...,S_q,...,S_p}$ do not exist in the choice situation, or if their existence is not accepted by the decision maker, then she or he can deal with only her or his goals, $\mathbf{G_1,...,G_j,...,G_n}$. In these circumstances, the responsible decision making model collapses into the rational choice model.

7.7 A Geometric Representation

Responsible decision making is stated by the maximin rule. It requires that the decision maker choose the decision alternative whose minimum value is the greatest in the multidimensional decision space of deontological, goal-achievement, and stakeholder values.

A simple geometrical representation might be helpful in visualizing the decision problem. Consider the cube depicted in Figure 14. The cube represents the decision space of deontological, goal-achievement, and stakeholder values. The values **D(A_i), G(A_i),** and **S(A_i)** are transformed into scales 0-1; so **D*(A_i), G*(A_i),** and **S*(A_i)** represent the different values of the decision alternative **Ai (0 ≤ D*(A_i), G*(A_i), S*(A_i) ≤ 1)**.

FIGURE 14
The Decision Space as Represented by a Cube

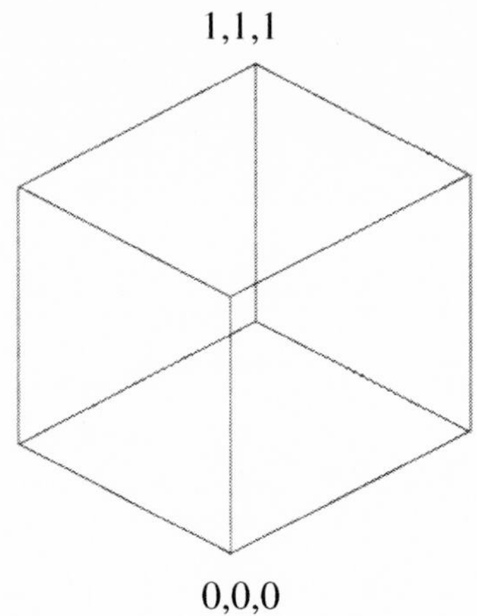

Decision alternatives are represented by particular points within the cube defined by parameters **D*(A_i), G*(A_i),** and **S*(A_i)**. The point **(0, 0, 0)** represents the worst possible decision alternative while point **(1,1,1)** represents the best possible decision alternative. The "goodness" of an actual decision alternative is represented by its distance from point **(1, 1, 1)**

The distance of decision alternative **A_i** from the ideal point **(1, 1, 1)** can be calculated by the following formula:

$$\delta\ (A_i) = \sqrt{[1 - D^*(A_i)] + [1 - G^*(A_i)] + [1 - S^*(A_i)]}$$

The decision alternative selected by responsible choice represents the minimal distance from the ideal point compared to the distances of other alternatives.

It should be observed that this geometric representation is not completely accurate because in the responsible choice model, values in distinct dimensions are not additive while values of the cube are additive. For this reason the geometric representation advanced here serves as an illustration only and not as a device for solving the problem.

However, there are also advantages of the geometrical representation. Decision makers may attribute different weights to the deontological, goal-achievement, and stakeholder value dimensions in actual decision situations. Their decision models can be represented by different rectangle boxes. Some examples are provided by Figure 15. Rectangle boxes can be considered modified forms of the cube that represents the ideal decision space in complex choice situations.

FIGURE 15
Modified Decision Spaces

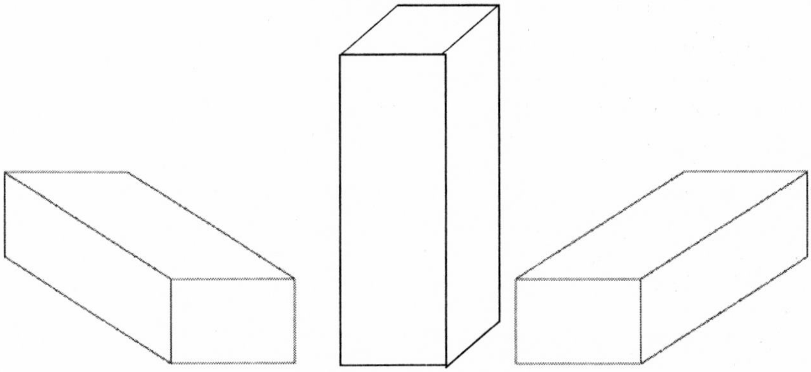

7.8 The Procedural Model

The procedural model of responsible decision making can be summarized as follows:

(I) Framing the choice situation by
  (i) identifying the applying ethical norms;
  (ii) mapping out the affected parties;
  (iii) defining goals and generating alternatives.

(II) Multiple evaluation of the available alternatives regarding
  (i) the ethical norms;
  (ii) the goals to be achieved; (iii) the affected parties.

(III) Finding the least worst alternative in the multidimensional space of deontological, goal-achievement, and stakeholder values.

There is always a conflict or at least some tension among the ethical norms, the agent's goals, and the interests of the stakeholders. Making a responsible choice is not at all easy. What is important is not eliminating the conflict but assuring some congruence among ethical norms, the agent's goals, and the interests of the stakeholders.

7.9 Summary

In complex choice situations, ethical norms apply that represent duties of the decision maker. The decision maker has goals that s/he wants to achieve in the choice situation. Finally, different stakeholders are present that can be affected by the outcome of the choice. Responsible decision making involves finding and implementing the decision alternative that realizes the idea of responsibility in the given context.

Deontological payoff is defined as the value of a decision alternative seen from the perspective of the applying ethical norms. The decision maker also considers the value of the decision alternatives from the perspective of the achievement of her/his goals. Stakeholders are present in complex choice situations, and the decision alternatives render different payoffs for them.

Deontological, goal-achievement, and stakeholder values together provide a multiple evaluation of the decision alternatives. Maintaining the complexity of the choice situation while trying to find an optimal balance among diverse value dimensions is a good strategy in complex choice situations.

The maximin rule can serve as a decision rule. It implies the maximization of the minimum payoff of decision alternatives. The rule is intuitively known by chess players. However, it was first described by Ernest Zermello and developed further by John von Neumann in his game theory.

Responsible decision making demands the selection of the least worst alternative in the decision space of deontological, goal-achievement, and stakeholder values, in the sense that the minimum value of the selected alternative is greater than the minimum value of any other alternative available for the decision maker in the given situation.

The underlying principle of responsible decision making is that the decision maker should find an optimal balance among the applying ethical norms, her or his own goals, and the interest of the stakeholders.

The responsible choice represents a Pareto optimal result in the multidimensional decision space. This means that given the set of decision alternatives, it is not possible to increase the payoff in one value dimension without decreasing it in at least one other value dimension. In this sense the alternative chosen by the maximin rule dominates all the other alternatives.

It is important to note that if ethical norms and stakeholders do not exist in the choice situation, or if their existence is not accepted by the decision maker, then the responsible decision making model collapses into the rational choice model.

The procedure for responsible decision making is as follows: (1) framing the choice situation by identifying the applying ethical norms; (2) mapping out the affected parties, defining goals and generating alternatives; (3) using multiple evaluation of the available alternatives regarding the ethical norms, the goals to be achieved, and the affected parties; and (4) finding the least worst alternative in the multidimensional space of deontological, goal-achievement, and stakeholder values.

Some congruence among ethical norms, the agent's goals, and the interests of the stakeholders should be assured in order to arrive at a responsible decision.

8. Real World Cases

In this chapter complex cases are presented and analyzed with the help of the responsible decision making framework. The main function of the exercise is to show how the model can work in real life situations.

Section 8.1 presents the case of Donna, who wants to prevent the beating of her friend Ali by a gang of racists in London. However, she can do it only if she breaks an ethical norm that defends the privacy of a third party.

Section 8.2 introduces the famous case of the Ford Pinto, in which one of the largest American car manufacturers neglected its responsibility to produce and sell cars that were "safe enough" for its customers. This irresponsible policy resulted in deaths and serious injuries of people who bought the Pinto. It is an old case and much have been written about it but the responsible decision making framework can give some new insights in the ethical structure of the case.

Section 8.3 analyzes the case of the World Bank environmental policy. A policy option was considered stating that the bank should encourage more migration of dirty industry to less developed countries. By adopting such a policy the World Bank could violate the fundamental norm of fairness and well as produce negative payoffs for major stakeholder groups.

These analyses give new insights into the moral structure of the selected complex choice situations.

8.1 Donna's Case

Amartya Sen has developed an illustrative moral problem in which conflicting ethical norms and diverse stakeholder interests are present in an intermingled way (Sen, A. 1982: pp 191-192.).

Ali is a successful shopkeeper who quickly built up a good business in London after emigrating from East Africa. He is, however, hated by a small group of local racists, and a particular gang of them plans to beat up Ali that evening in some secluded spot to which Ali will go alone. Donna, a West Indian friend of Ali's, has just learned of the bashers' plan and wants to warn Ali about it. Ali has gone away for the day, and will go to the secluded spot without returning home. Donna does not know where Ali has gone, nor does she know the location of the planned beating, but she does know that Ali has left a message on the desk of his business contact, Charles, concerning his whereabouts. However, Charles is away for the day also and cannot be contacted. Hence the only way of getting Ali's message is by breaking into Charles' room. Donna asked for help from the police, who dismissed Donna's story as a piece of paranoiac fantasy. Donna knows that she can certainly frustrate the planned beating by breaking into Charles' room, recovering the message, and warning Ali during the day. But she cannot do this without violating the privacy of Charles, who, Donna also knows, is a secretive man who will feel embarrassed at the thought of someone looking through his personal papers to find the message. Donna also knows that Charles is a self-centered egoist who will be more perturbed by the violation of his privacy than by the beating of Ali. What should Donna do?

If Donna wants to make a responsible decision she should analyze the situation from multiple value-perspectives.

Two alternatives are available for Donna:

$\mathbf{A_1}$ = breaking into Charles' room and saving Ali
$\mathbf{A_2}$ = revering Charles' privacy and not saving Ali

In the choice situation, the applying ethical norm is "helping your friend in danger," while the other ethical norm is the "reverence for one's privacy" ($\mathbf{D_1}$ and $\mathbf{D_2}$, respectively). Donna's main goal **G** is to "save Ali by informing him about the bashers' plan." The stakeholders are Ali ($\mathbf{S_1}$), Charles ($\mathbf{S_2}$), and the bashers ($\mathbf{S_3}$).

The deontological values of decision alternative $\mathbf{A_1}$ are as follows:

$$\mathbf{D_1(A_1) = 1}$$
$$\mathbf{D_2(A_1) = -2}$$

Breaking into Charles' office and saving Ali in this way corresponds to ethical norm $\mathbf{D_1}$ but violates ethical norm $\mathbf{D_2}$.

Decision alternative $\mathbf{A_1}$ is positive for the achievement of Donna's main goal **G**. So the goal-achievement value of $\mathbf{A_1}$ is as follows:

$$\mathbf{G(A_1) = 1}$$

The stakeholder payoffs of decision alternative A_1 are as follows:

$$\mathbf{S_1(A_1) = 1}$$
$$\mathbf{S_2(A_1) = -2}$$
$$\mathbf{S_3(A_1) = -2}$$

$\mathbf{A_1}$ is good for Ali but bad for Charles and also bad for the would-be attackers.

To get an overall picture about $\mathbf{A_1}$ we should aggregate the deontological values as well as the stakeholder values.

Let $\mathbf{w_1}$ and $\mathbf{w_2}$ be weights reflecting the relative importance of ethical norms $\mathbf{D_1}$ and $\mathbf{D_2}$, respectively ($\mathbf{0 < w_1, w_2 < 1}$ and $\mathbf{w_1 + w_2 = 1}$).

Hence the aggregate deontological value of $\mathbf{A_i}$ can be calculated as

$$\mathbf{D(A_1) = w_1 \text{-} 2w_2}$$

Let $\mathbf{v_1}$, $\mathbf{v_2}$ and $\mathbf{v_3}$ be weights that reflect the relative importance of the stakeholders—Ali, Charles and the bashers, respectively. The stake of the bashers is not legitimate; consequently, $\mathbf{v_3 = 0}$. ($\mathbf{0 < v_1, v_2 < 1}$ and $\mathbf{v_1 + v_2 = 1}$)

Hence the aggregate stakeholder value of $\mathbf{A_1}$ can be calculated as

$$\mathbf{S(A_1) = v_1 \text{-} 2v_2}$$

Multiple evaluations of decision alternative $\mathbf{A_1}$ are provided by the following vector:

$$\mathbf{\underline{V}(A_1) = [w_1 \text{-} 2w_2, 1, v_1 \text{-} 2v_2]}$$

Decision alternative $\mathbf{A_2}$ presents the following deontological payoffs:

$$\mathbf{D_1(A_2) = -2}$$
$$\mathbf{D_2(A_2) = 1}$$

Using the same weights $\mathbf{w}_1$ and $\mathbf{w}_2$ we can arrive at

$$\mathbf{D(A_2) = w_2\text{-}2w_1}$$

Revering Charles' privacy is negative for the achievement of Donna's goal with certainty because in this case she cannot save Ali from the beating.

$$\mathbf{G(A_2) = \text{-}2}$$

Alternative $\mathbf{A}_i$ is bad for Ali, neutral for Charles, and good for the attackers.

$$\mathbf{S_1(A_2)= \text{-}2}$$
$$\mathbf{S_2(A_2) = 0}$$
$$\mathbf{S_3(A_2) = 1}$$

Using the same weights $\mathbf{v}_1$, $\mathbf{v}_2$ and $\mathbf{v}_3$ we can aggregate the stakeholder payoffs as follows:

$$\mathbf{S(A_2) = v_1\text{-}2\ v_1}$$

Multiple evaluations of decision alternative $\mathbf{A}_2$ are provided by the following vector:

$$\mathbf{\underline{V}(A_2)=[w_2\text{-}2w_1,\text{-}2,v_2\text{-}2v_1]}$$

Table 3 shows the payoffs in Donna's case.

TABLE 3
Payoffs in Donna's Original Case

	Deontological value	**Goal-achievement value**	**Stakeholder value**
A_1	w_1-$2w_2$	1	v_i-$2v_2$
A_2	w_2-$2w_1$	-2	v_2-$2v_1$

The responsible decision is $\mathbf{A_1}$ because

$$\mathbf{min\ [w_1\text{-}2w_2, 1, v_i\text{-}2v_2] > min\ [w_2\text{-}2w_1, \text{-}2, v_2\text{-}2v_1]}$$

It is held since the worst component of $\underline{\mathbf{V}}(\mathbf{A_2})$ is **-2**. The worst component of $\underline{\mathbf{V}}(\mathbf{A_1})$ is greater than **-2** holding that $\mathbf{0 < w_1}$ and $\mathbf{0 < v_1}$.

Donna has a good reason for breaking into Charles' office and trying to warn Ali about the planned beating. It is even required of her if she wants to solve the problem as a responsible person. This result is consistent with Amartya Sen's own analysis (Sen, A. 1982).

Sen has generated some variants of the original case. One of these variants is especially interesting.

> In particular, the so-called bashers are not bashers really; in fact they work in Ali's shop. (Ali calls them bashers since he is liable to complain that they handle the merchandise clumsily.) The bashers suspect that they have been given a more dismal picture about the firm's financial position than is justified by accountants, and they want to examine the accounts without Ali's permission in Ali's absence. Donna has come to know of this, and is considering warning Ali about this likely occurrence, which will have, Donna knows, bad consequences for Ali's business plans. But she can warn Ali only by breaking into Charles' room (Sen, A. 1982: p. 202.).

The two alternatives now consist of the following:

$\mathbf{A_1}$* = breaking into Charles' office in order to inform Ali about the planned financial examination of the "bashers"

$\mathbf{A_2}$* = revering Charles' privacy and not informing Ali about the planned financial examination of the "bashers"

Now just one ethical norm applies; namely, "reverence for one's privacy": **(D)** Informing Ali about the planned violation of his business secret might be a virtuous act but certainly is not a duty of Donna's.

$$\mathbf{D(A_1^*) = -2}$$
$$\mathbf{D(A_2^*) = 1}$$

Donna wants to help Ali in this case too: **(G)** Alternative $\mathbf{A_1}$* serves her goal with certainty. Alternative $\mathbf{A_2}$* is negative for Donna's goal achievement with certainty.

$$\mathbf{G(A_1^*) = 1}$$
$$\mathbf{G(A_2^*) = -2}$$

Stakeholders are the same as in the original case: Ali (**S_1**), Charles (**S_2**), and the bashers (**S_3**). The stakeholder payoffs and weights are also the same.

$$\mathbf{S(A_1^*) = v_1 - 2v_2}$$
$$\mathbf{S(A_2^*) = v_2 - 2v_1}$$

Multiple evaluations of alternative Aj* and A_2* are provided by the following vectors:

$$\mathbf{\underline{V}(A_1^*) = [-2, 1, v_1 - 2v_2]}$$
$$\mathbf{\underline{V}(A_2^*) = [1, -2, v_2 - 2v_1]}$$

Table 4 shows the payoffs in Donna's modified case.

TABLE 4
Payoffs in Donna's Modified Case

	Deontological value	**Goal-achievement value**	**Stakeholder value**
A_1*	–2	1	V_1-2v_2
A_2*	1	–2	v_2-2v_1

It holds that

$$\mathbf{\min V(A_2^*) > \min V(A_1^*)}$$

since the worst components of the two vectors are equal but the second worst component of **$\underline{V}$**(A_2*) is **better** than that of **$\underline{V}$**(A_j*), presupposing that $v_1 < v_2$.

This means that alternative **A_2***is the responsible decision for Donna, assuming that Charles' privacy has greater weight than Ali's warning about the bashers' financial inspection.

8.2 The Ford Pinto Case

The following is one incident that was reported:

> On August 10, 1978, a tragic automobile accident occurred on US Highway 33 near Goshen, Indiana. Sisters Judy and Lynn Ulrich (ages 18 and 16, respectively) and their cousin Donna Ulrich (age 18) were struck from the rear in their 1973 Ford Pinto by a van. The gas tank of the Pinto ruptured, the car burst into flames, and the three teenagers were burned to death (Hoffman, M.W. 1984: p. 552.).

This was not the only case where the Ford Pinto caused serious accidents by explosion. There were many lawsuits filed against Ford after it was proven that the top managers of the company had been informed about the design problem of the model. Despite the warnings of their engineers, Ford management decided to manufacture and sell the car.

Our ethical intuition suggests that the Ford managers acted in a nonresponsible way because they decided to put an unsafe model on the market. How can the case be framed in the responsible choice model?

The main goal of Ford managers was not to lose market position and profit. This goal **G** is the only one in the choice situation. Notice that during the 1970s, the Pinto was one of the most successful Ford models. Although it sold well, it was undergoing serious competition from Volkswagen in the market for smaller cars.

The most relevant ethical norm is that of supplying safe products to customers and avoid jeopardizing their lives. ($\mathbf{D_j}$) However, another ethical norm also applies, namely to inform the customers about the possible dangers of the product ($\mathbf{D_2}$).

The stakeholders are the actual users of the car ($\mathbf{S_1}$) and the potential buyers of the car ($\mathbf{S_2}$), including their families.

Basically two decision alternatives were available to the Ford managers.

$\mathbf{A_1}$ = manufacturing and selling the car without modification;
$\mathbf{A_2}$ = modifying the model and introducing the safer version;

Ford engineers concluded that the safety problem of the Pinto could be solved by a minor technological improvement costing only **$11** per car. However, Ford produced a cost-benefit analysis regarding the modification that concluded it would not be cost effective for society. The result of this intriguing and controversial study is shown in Table 5.

TABLE 5
The Ford Cost-Benefit Analyses Study

	Benefits
Savings	180 burn deaths,
	180 serious burn injuries,
	2,100 burned vehicles
Unit cost	$200,000 per death,
	$67,000 per injury,
	$700 per vehicle
Total benefit	180 x $200,000 +
	180 x $67,000 +
	2,100 x $700
	= $49.5 million
	Costs
Sales	11 million cars,
	1 .5 million light trucks
Unit cost	$11 per car,
	$11 per truck
Total cost	$11x11,000,000 +
	$11 x 1,500,000
	= $137 million

Source: Hoffman, M.W. 1984: pp. 554-555.

Decision alternative $\mathbf{A}_1$ violates both ethical norms $\mathbf{D}_1$ and $\mathbf{D}_2$.

It was stated by experts that the Pinto was not as safe as comparable cars with regard to the positioning of its gas tank. Leslie Ball, the founder of the International Society of Reliability Engineers, determined, "The release to production of the Pinto was the most reprehensible decision in the history of American engineering." He was able to name more than 40 European and Japanese models in the Pinto price and weight range with safer gas tank positioning. Los Angeles auto safety expert Byron Block said that the Pinto fuel system was a catastrophic blunder. He concluded, "Ford made an extremely irresponsible decision when they placed such a weak tank in such a ridiculous location in such a soft rear end. It is almost designed to blow up—premeditated" (Hoffman, M.W. 1984: p. 554).

In addition, Ford did not inform their customers and the general public about the safety problem of the Pinto, even though it was internally reported by their engineers years before the first accidents happened.

$$\mathbf{D_1(A_1) = -2}$$
$$\mathbf{D_2(A_1) = -2}$$

Decision alternative $\mathbf{A_1}$ serves the main goal of Ford.

$$\mathbf{G(A_1) = 1}$$

Decision alternative $\mathbf{A_1}$ is unquestionably bad for both groups of stakeholders.

$$\mathbf{S_1(A_1) = -2}$$
$$\mathbf{S_2(A_1) = -2}$$

The aggregate deontological, goal-achievement, and stakeholder values of decision alternative $\mathbf{A_1}$ are as follows:

$$\mathbf{\underline{V}(A_1) = [-2, 1, -2]}$$

Here it does not matter which weights are used in aggregating deontological and stakeholder values since the numerical values are the same.

Decision alternative $\mathbf{A_2}$ corresponds to both ethical norms $\mathbf{D_1}$ and $\mathbf{D_2}$.

$$\mathbf{D_1(A_2) = 1}$$
$$\mathbf{D_2(A_2) = 1}$$

Modifying the model and introducing the safer version would have influenced the market position and profits of Ford; however, they did not launch any serious research about this alternative. So decision alternative A_2 can be considered as negative regarding the main goal of Ford.

$$G(A_2) = -2$$

Modifying the model and introducing the safer version is good for both groups of stakeholders. The price-incensement ($11) is very small in comparison to the avoidance of risking a catastrophe.

$$S_1(A_2) = 1$$
$$S_2(A_2) = 1$$

The aggregate deontological, goal-achievement, and stakeholder values of decision alternative A_2 are as follows:

$$\underline{V}(A_2) = [1, -2, 1]$$

Table 6 shows the multiple payoffs of the decision alternatives in the Ford Pinto case.

TABLE 6
Payoffs in the Ford Pinto Case

	Deontological value	Goal-achievement value	Stakeholder value
A_1 alternative	-2	1	-2
A_2 alternative	1	-2	1

It is easy to see that the responsible decision is A_2; that is, modifying the model and introducing the safer version.

It holds that

$$\min \underline{V}(A_2) > \min \underline{V}(A_1)$$

since the worst payoff of alternative A_1 is **-2** and the worst payoff of alternative A_2 is also **-2** but the second worst payoff of A_2 is greater than that of $\mathbf{A}_1$ (**1** versus **-2**). According to the maximin rule, alternative $\mathbf{A}_2$ dominates alternative $\mathbf{A}_1$.

In the actual case, Ford managers followed the moral disengagement strategy by choosing the alternative of manufacturing and selling the car without modification (Bandura, A. et al. 1996, Bandura, A., G-V. Caprara, and L. Zsolnai 2000). Ford managers displaced their responsibility with reference to US federal safety standards, disregarded the consequences of their action, and used their cost-benefit analysis as moral justification for their reprehensible conduct.

8.3 The World Bank Environmental Policy

Daniel M. Hausman and Michael S. McPherson cite a provocative case concerning the World Bank environmental policy (Hausman, D.M. and McPherson, M.S. 1996: pp. 9-10):

> In December of 1991, *Lawrence Summers,* who was then the chief economist at the World Bank, sent the following memorandum to some colleagues: Just between you and me, should not the World Bank be encouraging more migration of dirty industries *to LDCs* (less developed countries)? (1) The measurement of the costs of health-impairing pollution depends on the foregone earnings from increased morbidity and mortality. From this point of view a given amount of health-impairing pollution should be done in the country with the lowest cost, which will be the country with the lowest wages. I think the economic logic behind dumping a load of toxic waste in the lowest-wage country is impeccable and we should face up to that. (2) The costs of pollution are likely to be non-linear as the initial increments of pollution probably have very low cost. I have always thought that under-populated countries in Africa are vastly *under* polluted. Only the lamentable facts that so much pollution is generated by non-tradable industries (transport, electrical generation) and that the unit transport costs of solid waste are so high prevent world-welfare-enchanting trade in air pollution and waste. (3) The demand for a clean environment for aesthetic and health reasons is likely to have very high income-elasticity. The concern over an agent that causes a one-in-a-million in the odds of the prostate cancer is obviously going to be much higher in a country where people survive to get prostate cancer than in a country where under-5 mortality is 200 per thousand. Also, much of the concern over industrial atmospheric discharge is about visibility-impairing particulates. These discharges may have very little health impact. Clearly, trade in goods that embody aesthetic pollution concerns could be welfare-enchanting. While production is mobile the consumption of pretty air is a non-tradable (Quoted in *The Economist*, February 8, 1992, p. 66).

The case has a rich variety of stakeholders because not only citizens of developed and less-developed countries can be affected by the World

Bank environmental policy but also the natural environment and future generations.

The policy options, or the alternatives, are as follows:

A_1 = encouraging the migration of dirty industries to LDCs
A_2 = not encouraging the migration of dirty industries to LDCs

The most relevant ethical norm that applies here is "fairness" (**D**). It can be formulated as the pay-your-way principle, which requires locating "polluting industries so that those who derive the largest benefits from industries endure most of the pollution costs" (Hausman, D.M. & McPherson, M.S. 1996: p. 204.).

The declared goal of the World Bank is to enhance global welfare (**G**).

The most important stakeholders can be identified as citizens of the developed countries (S_1), dirty industries in the developed countries (S_2), citizens of the less-developed countries (S_3), the natural environment affected by dirty industries in the developed countries (S_4), the targeted natural environment in the less-developed countries (S_5), and future generations (S_6).

From a deontological value perspective, alternative A_1 is certainly negative while alternative A_2 is certainly positive because the latter corresponds to the norm of fairness and the former violates it.

$$D(A_1) = -2$$
$$D(A_2) = 1$$

Alternative A_1 serves the goal of enhancing global welfare with probability **p**. Alternative A_2 is negative for this goal with probability **q**. Notice that **p+q** is not necessarily equal to 1 since it is possible that global welfare is neither increased nor decreased by encouraging the migration of dirty industries to LDCs.

$$G(A_1) = 3p-2$$
$$G(A_2) = 1-3q$$

The stakeholder payoffs of the alternative AI can be calculated as follows:

$$\mathbf{S_1(A_1) = 1}$$
$$\mathbf{S_2(A_1) = 1}$$
$$\mathbf{S_3(A_1) = -2}$$
$$\mathbf{S_4(A_1) = 1}$$
$$\mathbf{S_5(A_1) = -2}$$
$$\mathbf{S_6(A_1) = -2}$$

Migration of dirty industries to LDCs would be good for the citizens of developed countries, for the industries themselves, and for the natural environment affected by those industries in the developed countries. However, it would be bad for the citizens of less-developed countries, for the targeted natural environment in the less-developed countries, and for future generations since environmental pollution is much more controllable in the developed countries than in the less-developed countries.

The stakeholder payoffs of alternative $\mathbf{A_2}$ can be calculated as follows:

$$\mathbf{S_1(A_2) = 0}$$
$$\mathbf{S_2(A_2) = 0}$$
$$\mathbf{S_3(A_2) = 0}$$
$$\mathbf{S_4(A_2) = 0}$$
$$\mathbf{S_5(A_2) = 0}$$
$$\mathbf{S_6(A_1) = 1}$$

This policy option is neutral for all the stakeholders except future generations, who would benefit from keeping dirty industries in the developed countries by forcing them to innovate and to become more environmentally friendly.

The question is how to weight stakeholders $\mathbf{S_1,..,S_6}$. Let $\mathbf{v_1,..,v_6}$ be importance weights attributed to the stakeholders.

It can be argued that equal weights should be attributed to nature, society, and future generations. This implies that $\mathbf{v_1 + v_2 + v_3 = v_4 + v_5 = v_6}$. We cannot discriminate between citizens of the developed countries and citizens of the less-developed countries, consequently $\mathbf{v_1 = v_3}$. Similarly, we cannot discriminate between the natural environment in the developed countries and the natural environment in the less-developed countries, consequently $\mathbf{v_4 = v_5}$. Considering all the stockholders, employees, and customers served by dirty industries,

they can get a somewhat similar weight as citizens of the developed countries: $v_1 = v_2$.
It is required that

$$\sum v_i = 1 \qquad (i = 1,...,6)$$

Hence we arrive at

$$v_1 = 0.11;\ v_2 = 0.11;\ v_3 = 0.11;\ v_4 = 0.17;\ v_5 = 0.17;\ v_6 = 0.33$$

Aggregate stakeholder payoffs of the two policy options are calculated as follows:

$$S(A_1) = -0.83$$
$$S(A_2) = 0.33$$

Multiple evaluations of the alternatives are provided by the following vectors:

$$V(A_1) = [-2, 3p-2, -0.83]$$
$$V(A_2) = [1, 1-3q, 0.33]$$

Table 7 shows the different payoffs of the two policy options.

TABLE 7
Payoffs in the World Bank Case

	Deontological value	Goal-achievement value	Stakeholder value
A_1	-2	3p-2	-0.83
A_2	1	1-3q	0.33

According to the maximin rule, A_2 dominates A_1. The World Bank should not encourage migration of dirty industries to less-developed countries. This would hold true even if citizens of the less-developed countries were to get full monetary compensation from citizens of the developed countries.

8.4 Summary

In Donna's case the responsible decision is to break into Charles' office and try to warn Ali about the planned assault. This is less worse than respecting the privacy of Charles while allowing Ali to be beaten by the racist gang.

In the Ford Pinto case, the responsible decision would be modifying the car and introducing the safer version to the market. This action would serve the interest of the stakeholders and correspond to the relevant ethical norms.

In the World Bank environmental policy case, certainly the bank should not encourage migration of dirty industries to less developed countries. Some questionable welfare improvement cannot compensate for the violation of the norm of fairness as well as jeopardizing the health of major groups of people.

9. Applications in Economics and Public Policy

In this chapter the responsible decision making framework is used to discuss some fundamental problems of economics and public policy.

In Section 9.1 John Rawls' famous principle of justice is defended on the basis of responsible choices made by people knowing perfectly their positions in society.

In Section 9.2 the so-called Paradox of a Paretian Liberal is discussed. It will be shown that the information provided by individual preferences might not be sufficient to formulate accurate public polices.

In Section 9.3 the Prisoners' Dilemma game is studied. It is demonstrated that unlike self-interested actions, responsible agency can lead to optimal outcomes in prisoners' dilemma situations.

In Section 9.4 the basic idea of cost-benefit analysis is reformulated in the multidimensional decision space that includes environmental, monetary, and social values.

In Section 9.5 the ethical and social acceptability of profit making is studied, while in Section 9.6 the problem of establishing justice among nature, society, and future generations is investigated.

9.1 Responsibility and Social Justice

In his masterpiece *A Theory of Justice,* John Rawls formulates the conception of justice as follows (Rawls, J. 1971: p. 60 and p. 83):

(I) "Each person has an equal right to a fully adequate scheme of equal basic rights and liberties compatible with a similar scheme for everyone.

(II) "Social and economic inequalities are to be arranged so that they are:
  (a) attached to positions and offices open to all under of fair equality of opportunity;
  (b) to the greatest benefit of the least advantaged."

Section II(b) is called the "difference principle," which is a well-known application of the maximin rule.

Rawls argues that in the hypothetical "original position"—where parties are mutually disinterested moral persons who make their choices under the "veil of ignorance," having no knowledge about their individual places in society—people rationally choose the conception of justice described by (I) and (II).

Even if it is very influential, Rawls' conception of justice has been criticized on diverse grounds. For example, John Harsanyi argues that rational individuals would not accept the difference principle because it is risk averse (Harsanyi, J. 1975).

Harsanyi may or may not be right. What is important for us is to show that responsible persons would accept the difference principle in the actual position, where each of them knows perfectly well her or his own place in society.

Imagine a society that consists of three individuals: **N, A,** and **B**. **N** is a normal, average person; A is an above-average person while B is a below-average person.

There are two alternatives for each person:

(Yes) Accepting the difference principle;
(No) Rejecting the difference principle.

N, A, and **B** can evaluate the two alternatives from deontological, goal-achievement and stakeholder perspectives.

From a deontological perspective, the difference principle can be judged as positive.

$$\mathbf{D(Yes) = 1}$$
$$\mathbf{D(No) = -2}$$

The goals of **N, A,** and **B** are to promote their own welfare in society ($\mathbf{G_1}$,$\mathbf{G_2}$, and $\mathbf{G_3}$, respectively).

The acceptance of the difference principle favors the goal achievement of **B** but disfavors the goal achievement of **N** and **A**.

$$G_1(\text{Yes}) = -2$$
$$G_2(\text{Yes}) = -2$$
$$G_3(\text{Yes}) = 1$$

The rejection of the difference principle favors the goal achievement of **N** and **A** but disfavors the goal achievement of **B**.

$$G_1(\text{No}) = 1$$
$$G_2(\text{No}) = 1$$
$$G_3(\text{No}) = -2$$

The stakeholder values of the two alternatives are similar to the goal-achievement values.

$$S_1(\text{Yes}) = -2$$
$$S_2(\text{Yes}) = -2$$
$$S_3(\text{Yes}) = 1$$

and

$$S_1(\text{No}) = 1$$
$$S_2(\text{No}) = 1$$
$$S_3(\text{No}) = -2$$

For person N the multiple evaluation of the two alternatives is as follows:

$$N(\text{Yes}) = [1, -2, -2w_i+w_2]$$
$$N(\text{No}) = [-2, 1, w_1-2w_2]$$

where $\mathbf{w}_1$ and $\mathbf{w}_2$ are weights that represent the relative stakes of A and B in accepting or rejecting the difference principle ($\mathbf{w}_1 + \mathbf{w}_2 = 1$).

Person **B**, who is below average, certainly has a greater stake concerning the difference principle than person A, who is above average. So $\mathbf{w}_2 > 0.5$ and $\mathbf{w}_1 < 0.5$.

Hence

$$\textbf{min N(Yes)} > \textbf{min N(No)}$$

because $\mathbf{-2w_1 + w_2 > wi -2w_2}$.

N as a responsible person will accept the difference principle. Now let us turn to person A. The multiple evaluation of the alternatives for him or her is as follows:

$$\mathbf{A(Yes) = [1, -2, -2v_1+v_2]}$$
$$\mathbf{A(No) = [-2, 1, v_1-2v_2]}$$

where $\mathbf{v_1}$ and $\mathbf{v_2}$ are weights that represent the relative stakes of **N** and **B** in accepting or rejecting the difference principle ($\mathbf{v_1 + v_2 = 1}$).

Person **N** has a smaller stake concerning the difference principle than person **B**, so

$$\mathbf{v_1 < 0.5 \text{ and } v_2 > 0.5}$$

Hence

$$\textbf{min A(Yes)} > \textbf{min A(No)}$$

because $-\mathbf{2v_1 + v_2 > v_1 - 2v_2}$.

A as a responsible person will accept the difference principle. Finally, let us turn to person **B**. The multiple evaluation of the alternatives for her or him is as follows:

$$\mathbf{B(Yes) = [1,1,-2]}$$
$$\mathbf{B(No) = [-2,-2,1]}$$

Here

$$\textbf{min B(Yes)} > \textbf{min B(No)}$$

For this reason **B** as a responsible person will accept the difference principle.

The conclusion we can draw from this exercise is that responsible persons—who wish to make responsible decisions—will accept the difference principle regardless of their actual placements in society.

9.2 The Paradox of a Paretian Liberal

Amartya Sen has established a strong case that there is a conflict between liberalism and the Pareto principle (Sen, A. 1970).

Imagine two individuals, Lewd and Prude. Their shared problem is whether or not to read D.H. Lawrence's famous erotic novel *Lady Chatterley's Lover.*

There are four possible states of affairs in the situation:

(L&P)	both read the book
(P)	only Prude reads the book
(L)	only Lewd reads the book
(0)	neither reads the book

Lewd most prefers that both of them read *Lady Chatterley's Lover.* If only one could read the book, Lewd would wish that Prude read it, since it would loosen her or him up. If Prude will not read the book, then Lewd prefers to read it alone. For Lewd the least preferred state of affairs is that neither of them reads the book.

Lewd's preference ordering over the states of affairs is as follows:

$$\textbf{(L\&P)} \longrightarrow \textbf{(P)} \longrightarrow \textbf{(L)} \longrightarrow \textbf{(0)} \qquad \textbf{(9.1)}$$

Prude most prefers that neither of them reads *Lady Chatterley's Lover* but would rather read it alone than further Lewd's corruption. If Lewd alone would read the book is less worse for Prude than if both of them would read it.

Prude's preference ordering over the states of affairs is as follows:

$$\textbf{(0)} \longrightarrow \textbf{(P)} \longrightarrow \textbf{(L)} \longrightarrow \textbf{(L\&P)} \qquad \textbf{(9.2)}$$

Lewd prefers **(L&P)** to **(P)** and Prude prefers **(L)** to **(L&P)**, so if social choice respects minimal liberalism then the outcome should be **(L)**—that only Lewd reads the book. However, both Lewd and Prude prefer **(P)** to **(L)**, and the Pareto principle requires that **(P)**—only Prude reads the book—should be socially preferred to **(L)**. If both minimal liberalism and the Pareto principle are respected, then there is a cycle, and the problem cannot be solved (Hausman, D.M. & McPherson, M.S. 1996: pp. 175-176.).

The problem is called the "Paradox of a Paretian Liberal." In the literature there are many attempts to resolve the problem. However, it seems that the paradox is real. Sen himself argues that the main message of the paradox is that normative social policy cannot be based on individual preferences alone (Sen, A. 1992).

In evaluating the states of affairs, we can use deontological and stakeholder considerations in addition to individual preferences.

In the case of Lewd and Prude, one applying ethical norm is certainly "reverence for privacy" (D), in that everybody is free to make her or his own decision on reading or not reading *Lady Chatterley's Lover.*

From the deontological perspective we can evaluate the possible states of affairs as follows:

$$\begin{aligned} \mathbf{D(L\&P)} &= \mathbf{-2} \\ \mathbf{D(L)} &= \mathbf{1} \\ \mathbf{D(P)} &= \mathbf{-2} \\ \mathbf{D(0)} &= \mathbf{-2} \end{aligned}$$

Only **(L)** corresponds to the norm of reverence for privacy. All the other states of affairs violate this ethical norm.

The goal of Lewd is to have Prude loosen up **(G_L)**, while the goal of Prude is to prevent Lewd's further corruption **(G_P)**. From the perspective of the achievement of these goals, the states of affairs can be evaluated as follows:

$$\begin{aligned} \mathbf{G_L(L\&P)} &= \mathbf{1} \\ \mathbf{G_L(L)} &= \mathbf{-2} \\ \mathbf{G_L(P)} &= \mathbf{1} \\ \mathbf{G_L(0)} &= \mathbf{-2} \end{aligned}$$

and

$$\begin{aligned} \mathbf{G_P(L\&P)} &= \mathbf{-2} \\ \mathbf{G_P(L)} &= \mathbf{-2} \\ \mathbf{G_P(P)} &= \mathbf{1} \\ \mathbf{G_P(0)} &= \mathbf{1} \end{aligned}$$

In calculating the aggregate goal-achievement value of the states of affairs, equal weights are attributed to the goal of Lewd and the goal of Prude.

$$
\begin{aligned}
G(L\&P) &= 0.5(1) + 0.5(-2) &= -0.5\\
G(L) &= 0.5(-2) + 0.5(-2) &= -2\\
G(P) &= 0.5(1) + 0.5(1) &= 1\\
G(0) &= 0.5(-2) + 0.5(1) &= -0.5
\end{aligned}
$$

Both Lewd and Prude should be considered as stakeholders: S_L and S_P, respectively. From the stakeholder perspective we can evaluate the states of affairs as follows:

$$
\begin{aligned}
S_L(L\&P) &= 1\\
S_P(L) &= 1\\
S_P(P) &= -2\\
S_P(0) &= -2
\end{aligned}
$$

In calculating the aggregate stakeholder values of the states of affairs, equal weights are again attributed to both stakeholders.

$$
\begin{aligned}
S(L\&P) &= 0.5(1) + 0.5(-2) &= -0.5\\
S(L) &= 0.5(1) + 0.5(1) &= 0\\
S(P) &= 0.5(-2) + 0.5(-2) &= -2\\
S(0) &= 0.5(-2) + 0.5(0) &= 0
\end{aligned}
$$

Table 8 shows the payoffs in the Lewd and Prude case.

TABLE 8
Payoffs in the Lewd & Prude Case

	Norm-regarding perspective	Goal-achievement perspective	Stakeholder perspective
Both read the book	-2	-0.5	-0.5
Only Lewd reads it	1	-2	0.5
Only Prude reads it	-2	1	-2
Neither read it	-2	-0.5	-1

Multiple evaluations of the states of affairs are provided by the following vectors:

$$\underline{\mathbf{V}}(\mathbf{L\&P}) = [-2,-0.5,-0.5]$$
$$\underline{\mathbf{V}}(\mathbf{L}) = [1,-2,0.5]$$
$$\underline{\mathbf{V}}(\mathbf{P}) = [-2,1,-2]$$
$$\underline{\mathbf{V}}(\mathbf{0}) = [-2,-0.5,-1]$$

The worst payoff of each state of affairs is -2, but considering the second worst payoffs we arrive at

$$\min \underline{\mathbf{V}}(\mathbf{L}) > \min \underline{\mathbf{V}}(\mathbf{L\&P}) > \min \underline{\mathbf{V}}(\mathbf{0}) > \min \underline{\mathbf{V}}(\mathbf{P}) \qquad (9.3)$$

This implies the following social preference ordering:

$$(\mathbf{L}) \longrightarrow (\mathbf{L\&P}) \longrightarrow (\mathbf{0}) \longrightarrow (\mathbf{P}) \qquad (9.4)$$

The desirable state of affairs is that *only Lewd should read Lady Chatterley's Lover*. If both Lewd and Prude read the book, it is less undesirable than if neither of them reads it. However, the most undesirable state of affairs would be if only Prude reads the book.

The state of affairs wherein only Lewd reads the book is Pareto optimal in the sense that it is not possible to improve the state of affairs in one value dimension without decreasing its value in at least one of the other dimensions.

The main message of this exercise is that the information provided by individual preferences might not be sufficient to make an accurate social ordering over the states of affairs. Deontological and stakeholder considerations should also be used in social evaluation to get a more accurate picture of the states of affairs.

9.3 Responsible Agency in Prisoner's Dilemma Situations

Game theory studies strategic interactions among individuals where the payoffs depend not only on the agent's choice but also on the choices of others.

One of the most famous games studied by game theorists is the so-called prisoner's dilemma game. The name of the game derives from a story about two prisoners, **J** and **K**. The district attorney separately offers each prisoner the choice between confessing and not-confessing. The best outcome for **J** occurs if she or he confesses and **K** does not. The second-best outcome is if both refuse to confess. The third best is if both agree to confess. The worst outcome for **J** is if **K** confesses and she or he does not.

The payoffs of the game are shown in Table 9.

TABLE 9
The Prisoner's Dilemma Game

K J	**Cooperate**	**Noncooperate**
Cooperate	3 3	4 0
Noncooperate	0 4	2 2

The problem is that if each prisoner pursues her or his rational self-interest then it leads to noncooperation, which presents a suboptimal outcome ([**2, 2**] instead of [**3, 3**]).

The prisoner's dilemma game is interesting not only for its own sake. It represents problems of social cooperation, free-riding, and the provision of public good:

> Individuals deciding whether to contribute to the production of public good seem like players in an n-person prisoner's dilemma game. "Free-riding"—that is, enjoying the public good but not contributing to its provision—is best of all. Second best is enjoying the public good and contributing one's share. Third best is doing without the public good. Worst is having others free-ride on one's contribution (Hausman, D.M. & McPherson, M.S. 1996: P. 184).

The standard solution to the prisoner's dilemma game is based on the self-interest of the players. Other solutions—as noted by Jane Mansbridge—derive from love or duty:

> That is, they require one or more of the interacting parties either to make the other's good their own or to be committed to a principle or course of action that requires co-operation. (...) Feeling of sympathy and/or commitment can be thought of as changing the payoff matrix in a prisoner's dilemma by adding to the co-operator's payoff a good derived from knowing that the other has benefited (love) or knowing that one acted morally (duty). (...) One might also

make a co-operative move in order to avoid the ills of empathetic distress and moral guilt (Mansbridge, J. 1990: pp. 135-136).

In reality people do not always maximize their self-interests as prescribed by standard game theory. People tend to cooperate in prisoner's dilemma situations in many real world cases. In a series of well-designed experiments, Dawes, van de Kragt, and Orbell found that a high percentage of American college students chose to act cooperatively and against their own self-interest. Dawes and his colleagues distinguished between "we-feeling" and "conscience," demonstrating that both motivations are separately at work (Dawes, R.M.; van de Kragt, A.J.C. and Orbell, R.M. 1990).

In light of the responsible decision making model, the possible strategies in the prisoner's dilemma game can be reevaluated.

There are two possible strategies for player **J**:

$$
\begin{aligned}
(\mathbf{C}) &= \text{cooperation} \\
(\sim\mathbf{C}) &= \text{noncooperation}
\end{aligned}
$$

These strategies can be evaluated from deontological, goal-achievement, and stakeholder perspectives.

We can consider cooperation as norm-fulfillment and noncooperation as norm-violation. Hence the deontological values of the strategies are as follows:

$$
\begin{aligned}
\mathbf{D(C)} &= \mathbf{1} \\
\mathbf{D(\sim C)} &= \mathbf{-2}
\end{aligned}
$$

The goal-achievement values of the strategies for player J can be calculated as follows:

$$
\begin{aligned}
\mathbf{G_j(C)} &= \mathbf{p(0.5) + (1\text{-}p)(\text{-}2) = 2.5p\text{-}2} \\
\mathbf{G_j(\sim C)} &= \mathbf{p(1) + (1\text{-}p)(0) = p}
\end{aligned}
$$

where p is the probability that the other player, **K**, cooperates $(\mathbf{0 \leq p \leq 1})$.

Considering the player **K** as a stakeholder of player **J**, the stakeholder values of the strategies can be calculated as follows:

$$S_k(C) = p(0.5) + (l\text{-}p)(l) = 1\text{-}O.Sp$$
$$S_k(\sim C) = p(-2) + (l\text{-}p)(0) = -2p$$

where p is again the probability that the other player K cooperates. Table 10 shows the multiple payoffs in the game.

TABLE 10
Reevaluated Payoffs in the Prisoner's Dilemma Game

K / J	Cooperate	Noncooperate
Cooperate	[1,0.5,0.5] [1,0.5,0.5]	[-2,1, -2] [1,-2,1]
Noncooperation	[1,-2,1] [-2,1, -2]	[-2, 0, 0] [-2, 0, 0]

The following vectors represent the multiple evaluation of the strategies for player J.

$$\underline{V}(C) = [1, 2.5p\text{-}2, l\text{-}0.5p]$$
$$\underline{V}(\sim C) = [-2, p, -2p]$$

As a responsible agent, player J uses the maximin rule in choosing his or her strategy:

$$\min \underline{V}(C) > \min \underline{V}(\sim C) \quad (9.5)$$

is held since the worst payoff of the cooperative strategy **(2.5p-2)** is greater than the worst payoff of the non cooperative strategy **(-2)** if $\mathbf{p > 0}$. If $\mathbf{p = 0}$, then the worst payoffs become equal **(-2)**, but the second worst payoff of the cooperative strategy is greater than that of the noncooperative strategy (**1** versus **0**).

Applying the maximin rule, the cooperative strategy pays better than the noncooperative strategy does. Since the game is symmetrical, for player **K** the cooperative strategy also pays better in the multidimensional evaluation space than the noncooperative strategy. In this way ethical decision making can lead to optimal outcomes in prisoner's dilemma situations. What self-interested players are not able to reach can be realized by responsible agents.

9.4 Multidimensional Cost-Benefit Analysis

The underlying idea of cost-benefit analysis is that a project is worthy of being undertaken if and only if the state of affairs with the project is better than the state of affairs without the project.

Monetary cost-benefit analysis does well in project evaluations if environmental and social externalities are not present and uncertainty is not involved. When externalities and uncertainty are present, monetary cost-benefit analysis may provide misleading results and can lead to bad policy recommendations.

Let **P** be a project whose total monetary cost is **P***. Let **Q** be the original state of affairs; that is, the state of affairs without the project. Let **Q*** be the new state of affairs; that is, the state of affairs with the project.

Let d(P) be the discounted cash flow that project **P** can produce for a given period of time. Let **d(P*)** be the discounted total earnings of the amount of money **P*** for the same period of time. In this way, **d(P)** and **d(P*)** represent two alternative uses for the same amount of money.

Let **E( )** and **S( )** be value functions by which the state of affairs can be evaluated from the ecological point of view and from the social point of view, respectively.

$$\mathbf{E(Q)} = \begin{cases} \mathbf{1} \text{ if the state of affairs } \mathbf{Q} \text{ is beneficial to nature;} \\ \mathbf{0} \text{ if the state of affairs } \mathbf{Q} \text{ is neutral to nature;} \\ \mathbf{-2} \text{ if the state of affairs } \mathbf{Q} \text{ is harmful to nature.} \end{cases} \quad (9.6)$$

For example, a motorway that cuts a natural ecosystem into two or more parts is certainly harmful to nature, whereas establishing a bioreserve might be beneficial.

$$\mathbf{S(Q)} = \begin{cases} \mathbf{1} \text{ if the state of affairs } \mathbf{Q} \text{ is good for society;} \\ \mathbf{0} \text{ if the state of affairs } \mathbf{Q} \text{ is neutral for society;} \\ \mathbf{-2} \text{ if the state of affairs } \mathbf{Q} \text{ is bad for society.} \end{cases} \quad (9.7)$$

For example, a well-functioning social security system is good for society while cutting back on the budgets of state universities might be bad for it.

Let **M( )** be a monetary value function as follows:

$$\mathbf{M(P)} = \begin{cases} \mathbf{1} \text{ if the discounted cash flow } \mathbf{d(P)} \text{ is positive;} \\ \mathbf{0} \text{ if the discounted cash flow } \mathbf{d(P)} \text{ is zero;} \\ \mathbf{-2} \text{ if the discounted cash flow } \mathbf{d(P)} \text{ is negative.} \end{cases} \quad (9.8)$$

Notice that **E(), S(),** and **M()** are Tversky-Kahneman type of value functions.

An overall evaluation of the state of affairs without the project is provided by the following vector:

$$\underline{\mathbf{V}}(\mathbf{Q} \ \& \ \mathbf{P^*}) = [\mathbf{E(Q)}, \mathbf{M(P^*)}, \mathbf{S(Q)}] \quad (9.9)$$

where **E(Q)** and **S(Q)** represent the environmental evaluation and the social evaluation of the original state of affairs and **M(P*)** represents the monetary evaluation of not undertaking the project.

Using the same **E( ), S( ),** and **M( )** value functions, the following vector provides an overall evaluation of the state of affairs with the project:

$$\mathbf{V}(\mathbf{Q^*} \ \& \ \mathbf{P}) = [\mathbf{E(Q^*)}, \mathbf{M(P)}, \mathbf{S(Q^*)}] \quad (9.10)$$

where **E(Q*)** and **S(Q*)** represent the environmental evaluation and social evaluation of the new state of affairs and **M(P)** represents the monetary evaluation of the project itself.

The necessary and sufficient condition for undertaking the project is that the following preference relation is held:

$$\underline{\mathbf{V}}(\mathbf{Q^*} \ \& \ \mathbf{P}) \longrightarrow \underline{\mathbf{V}}(\mathbf{Q} \ \& \ \mathbf{P^*}) \quad (9.11)$$

It means that the state of affairs with the project should be better than the state of affairs without the project considering environmental, monetary, and social values simultaneously.

(9.11) can be written as

$$[\mathbf{E(Q^*)}, \mathbf{M(P)}, \mathbf{S(Q^*)}] \longrightarrow [\mathbf{E(Q)}, \mathbf{M(P^*)}, \mathbf{S(Q^*)}] \quad (9.12)$$

How can we establish such a preference relation since the entities to be compared are multidimensional in nature?

Applying the maximin rule we get

$$\min [E(Q^*), S(Q^*), M(P)] > \min [E(Q), S(Q), M(P^*)] \quad (9.13)$$

If (9.13) is held then it means that the worst aspect of the new state of affairs is better than the worst aspect of the original state of affairs. If the environmental, social, and monetary aspects are considered as irreducible and equally important, then **Q* & P** should be preferred to **Q & P*** in the case of (7.13).

The irreducible complexity of resource allocation can be handled with the help of the maximin rule, which permits only limited tradeoffs among different values. The universal substitutability of values propagated by mainstream economics should be challenged.

The view of "market fundamentalism" criticized by George Soros is certainly wrong. Not every kind of value can be adequately translated into monetary terms. If a society were to let the market decide everything solely on the basis of expected profit or cash flow, then unconstrained market forces would destroy freedom, the richness of human culture, and the diversity of nature (Soros, G. 1998, McDaniel, C.D. and Gowdy, J. 2000).

The irreducible complexity of resource allocation can be handled with the help of the maximin rule that permits only limited tradeoffs among different values. The quality of life can be preserved and enhanced if decision makers pay equal attention to all the relevant value perspectives in the decision situation.

9.5 Ethical and Social Performance of Business

Since the birth of capitalism there has been an ongoing, passionate debate about the social and moral justification of profit making. In modern business ethics, the issue is formulated in terms of the social and ethical performance of business.

In empirical studies that try to assess the social and/or ethical performance of business organizations, deontological (norm-regarding) and stakeholder (other-regarding) aspects are often mixed up in a rather confusing way. Some conceptual clarification might be helpful.

I propose to define the ethical performance of a business organization on the basis of evaluating its activities from the perspective of the applying ethical norms. I propose to define the social performance of a business organization on the basis of evaluating its activities from the perspective of the stakeholders.

Considering these definitions, evaluation procedures can be developed to assess the ethical and social performance of business.

Let **B** be a business organization whose activities are $\mathbf{A_1,...,A_i,...,A_m}$ during a **period** of **time T** $(\mathbf{m} \geq 1)$. Let $\mathbf{D_1,...,D_k,...,D_p}$ be ethical norms that are relevant in judging the activities of the business organization during the period of time under consideration $(\mathbf{p \geq 0})$.

An ethical value function $\mathbf{D_k}(\ )$ can be defined as follows:

$$\mathbf{Dk}(\mathbf{A_i}) = \begin{cases} \mathbf{1} \text{ if activity } \mathbf{A_i} \text{ corresponds to ethical norm } \mathbf{D_k} \\ \mathbf{0} \text{ if activity } \mathbf{A_i} \text{ is neutral regarding ethical norm } \mathbf{D_k} \\ \mathbf{-2} \text{ if activity } \mathbf{A_i} \text{ violates ethical norm } \mathbf{D_k} \end{cases} \quad (9.14)$$

$\mathbf{D_k(A_i)}$ characteristically shows the value of activity $\mathbf{A_i}$ regarding ethical norm $\mathbf{D_k}$.

The following matrix reflects the ethical performance of business organization B during the time period T:

$$\mathbf{D(A)} = \begin{matrix} \mathbf{D_1(A_1),...,D_1(A_i),...,D_1(A_m)} \\ \mathbf{D_k(A_1),...,D_k(A_1),...,D_k(A_m)} \\ \mathbf{D_p(A_1),...,D_p(A_i),...,D_p(A_m)} \end{matrix} \quad (9.15)$$

To get an overall picture of the ethical performance of business organization B during time period T, we should introduce weights both for the activities and the ethical norms.

Let $\mathbf{x_i,...,x_j,...,x_m}$ be weights that reflect the relative importance of activities $\mathbf{A_1,...,A_i,...,A_m}$. Let $\mathbf{w_1,...,w_k,...,w_p}$ be weights that reflect the relative importance of ethical norms $\mathbf{D_1,...,D_k,...,D_p}$.

It is required that

$$\sum \mathbf{x_i = 1} \quad \text{and} \quad \sum \mathbf{w_k = 1} \qquad (9.16)$$

The ethical performance of business organization **B** during time period **T** can be calculated as follows:

$$\mathbf{D(A)} = \sum \sum \mathbf{w_k\, x_i\, D_k(A_i)} \qquad (9.17)$$

D(A) can be considered as a measure of ethical performance of business organization **B** during time period **T (1 ≥ D(A) ≥ -2).**

Let **P** be the profit or other relevant indicator of financial performance of business organization **B** during time period **T**.

P is ethically acceptable if and only if **D(A) > 0.** This means that business organization **B** produced its profit **P** during time period **T** by activities $\mathbf{A_1,\dots,A_i,\dots,A_m}$ that—in aggregate—do not violate ethical norms $\mathbf{D_1,\dots,D_k,\dots,D_p}$.

Now let us turn to the question of the social performance of business.

Let $\mathbf{S_1,\dots,S_q,\dots,S_r}$ be stakeholders that are affected by the activities $\mathbf{A_1,\dots,A_i,\dots,A_m}$ of business organization **B** during the period of time **T(r ≥ l)**.

A stakeholder value function $\mathbf{S_q()}$ can be defined as follows:

$$\mathbf{S_q(A_j)} = \begin{cases} \mathbf{1} \text{ if activity } \mathbf{A_i} \text{ is good for stakeholder } \mathbf{S_q} \\ \mathbf{0} \text{ if activity } \mathbf{A_i} \text{ is neutral for stakeholder } \mathbf{S_q} \\ \mathbf{-2} \text{ if activity } \mathbf{A_i} \text{ is bad for stakeholder } \mathbf{S_q} \end{cases} \qquad (9\text{-}18)$$

$\mathbf{S_q(A_j)}$ characteristically shows the value of activity Aj regarding stakeholder $\mathbf{S_q}$.

The following matrix reflects the social performance of business organization **B** during time period **T**.

$$\mathbf{S(A)} = \begin{matrix} \mathbf{S_1(A_1),\dots,S_1(A_1),\dots,S_1(A_m)} \\ \cdot \quad \cdot \quad \cdot \\ \mathbf{S_q(A_1),\dots,S_q(A_i),\dots,S_q(A_m)} \\ \cdot \quad \cdot \quad \cdot \\ \mathbf{S_r(A_1),\dots,S_r(A_i),\dots,S_r(A_m)} \end{matrix} \qquad (9.19)$$

To get an aggregate picture of the social performance of business organization **B** during the time period **T**, we should address weights to the stakeholders.

Let $\mathbf{v_1,\dots,v_q,\dots,v_r}$ be weights that reflect the relative importance of stakeholders $\mathbf{S_1,\dots,S_q,\dots,S_r}$. We can use the same weights $\mathbf{x_1,\dots,x_i,\dots,x_m}$ for the activities of the organization.

It is required that

$$\sum v_q = 1 \qquad (9.20)$$

The ethical performance of business organization **B** during time period **T** can be calculated as follows:

$$S(A) = \sum \sum v_q \text{ xi } S_q(A_i) \qquad (9.21)$$

S(A) can be considered as a measure of the social performance of business organization B during time period **T** $(1 \geq S(A) \geq -2)$.

Profit **P** is socially acceptable if and only if $S(A) > 0$. This means that business organization **B** produced its profit during period of time **T** by activities $A_1,...,A_i,...,A_m$ that—in aggregate—do not cause harm to stakeholders $S_1,...,S_q,...,S_r$.

Nonviolence, which is at the heart of economic ethics of many world religions, emerges as a necessary and sufficient condition for the ethical and social acceptability of profit making.

9.6 Nature, Society, and Future Generations

Any economic arrangement affects nature, society and future generations. An economic arrangement is hardly legitimate if it produces negative payoffs for these primordial stakeholders.

We can define value functions that evaluate economic arrangements from the perspective of nature, from the perspective of society, and from the perspective of future generations.

From the perspective of nature, the integrity of ecosystems is a central value. The notion of ecological integrity was first introduced by the American naturalist Aldo Leopold in his environmental classic *A Sand County Almanac*. He writes, "A thing is right when it tends to preserve the integrity, stability, and beauty of the biotic community. It is wrong when it tends otherwise" (Leopold, A. 1948: pp. 224-225.).

Economic arrangements can be evaluated against sustainability indicators that operationalize the notion of ecological integrity (Azar, C. et al. 1996).

Let **A** be an economic arrangement. Let $E_1,...,E_i,...,E_m$ be sustainability indicators $(m > 1)$.

$E_i(\,)$ is an ecological value function defined as follows:

$$\mathbf{E_i(A)} = \begin{cases} \mathbf{1} & \text{if economic arrangement } \mathbf{A} \text{ is good regarding sustainability indicator } \mathbf{E_i}; \\ \mathbf{0} & \text{if economic arrangement } \mathbf{A} \text{ is neutral regarding sustainability indicator } \mathbf{E_i}; \\ \mathbf{-2} & \text{if economic arrangement } \mathbf{A} \text{ is bad regarding sustainability indicator } \mathbf{E_i}. \end{cases} \tag{9.22}$$

$\mathbf{E_i(A)}$ reflects the ecological value of economic arrangement A regarding sustainability indicator $\mathbf{E_i}$.

The following vector represents the ecological value of economic arrangement A regarding all the sustainability indicators $\mathbf{E_1,...,E_i,...,E_m}$.

$$\underline{\mathbf{E}}\mathbf{(A) = [E_1(A),...,E_i(A),E_m(A)]} \tag{9.23}$$

To get an aggregate picture of the ecological value of an economic arrangement, we should define weights that reflect the relative importance of the sustainability indicators. Let $\mathbf{w_1,...,w_i,...,w_m}$ be such importance weights.

It is required that

$$\sum \mathbf{w_i = 1} \tag{9.24}$$

The aggregate ecological value of economic arrangement **A** can be calculated as follows:

$$\mathbf{E(A)} = \sum \mathbf{w_i E_i(A)} \tag{9.25}$$

E(A) reflects the aggregate ecological value of economic arrangement **A** $(\mathbf{1 \geq E(A) \geq -2})$.

Evaluating economic arrangements from a social perspective has been a long-lasting business of welfare economics. Here, well-being is the central value. However, well-being can be understood in different ways. Amartya Sen proposes that we understand well-being in terms of capabilities. Capability is primarily a reflection of the freedom of a person to achieve valuable functioning. Hence capabilities can be interpreted as substantive freedom that people enjoy (Sen, A. 1992: p. 49.).

Let $\mathbf{C_1,...,C_j,...,C_n}$ be capability indicators against which economic arrangements can be evaluated $(\mathbf{j > 1})$.

Let $\mathbf{C_j}(\ )$ social value function be defined as follows:

$$\mathbf{C_j(A)} = \begin{cases} \mathbf{1} & \text{if economic arrangement } \mathbf{A} \text{ is good regarding capability indicator } \mathbf{C_j}; \\ \mathbf{0} & \text{if economic arrangement } \mathbf{A} \text{ is neutral regarding capability indicator } \mathbf{C_j}; \\ \mathbf{-2} & \text{if economic arrangement } \mathbf{A} \text{ is bad regarding capability indicator } \mathbf{C_j}. \end{cases} \qquad (9.26)$$

$\mathbf{C_j(A)}$ reflects the social value of economic arrangement **A** regarding capability indicator $\mathbf{C_j}$.

The following vector represents the social value of economic arrangement A regarding all the capability indicators $\mathbf{C_1,..,C_j,...,C_n}$.

$$\underline{\mathbf{C}}\mathbf{(A) = [C_1(A),...,C_j(A),...,C_n(A)]} \qquad (9.27)$$

To get an aggregate picture of the social value of economic arrangement **A**, we should introduce **weights** that reflect the relative importance of the capability indicators. Let $\mathbf{u_j,...,u_j,...,u_n}$ be such importance weights.

It is required that

$$\sum \mathbf{u_j = 1} \qquad (9.28)$$

The aggregate social value of economic arrangement A can be calculated as follows:

$$\mathbf{C(A)} = \sum \mathbf{u_j\ C_j(A)} \qquad (9.29)$$

C(A) reflects the aggregate social value of economic arrangement **A** $\mathbf{(1 \geq C(A) \geq -2)}$.

The forms of (9.25) and (9.29) assure that the aggregate ecological value and the aggregate social value of economic arrangement **A** are comparable.

A balance between nature and society is established if

$$\mathbf{S(A) \approx C(A)} \qquad (9.30)$$

This means that the economic arrangement produces approximately equal values for nature and for society.

Notice that nature and society do not necessarily represent zero-sum or even constant-sum games. Economic arrangements may present "win-win," "win-lose," "lose-win" or "lose-lose" situations for nature and society. While preindustrial economies typically presented win-win situations, our industrial economies present lose-win or even lose-lose situations for nature and society.

How can economic arrangements be evaluated from the perspective of future generations?

According to Edith Brown Weiss, the freedom of future generations can be assured by satisfying the following principles (Brown Weiss, E. 1989):

(i) conservation of options;
(ii) conservation of quality;
(iii) conservation of access.

Considering principles (i),(ii), and (iii), future-generations indicators can be created. Let $\mathbf{F_1,...,F_k,...,F_p}$ be such indicators against which economic arrangements can be evaluated $\mathbf{(p > 1)}$.

Future-generations value function $\mathbf{F_k()}$ is defined as follows:

$$\mathbf{F_k(A)} = \begin{cases} \mathbf{1} & \text{if economic arrangement } \mathbf{A} \text{ is good regarding future-generations indicator } \mathbf{F_k}; \\ \mathbf{0} & \text{if economic arrangement } \mathbf{A} \text{ is neutral regarding future-generations indicator } \mathbf{F_k}; \\ \mathbf{-2} & \text{if economic arrangement } \mathbf{A} \text{ is bad regarding future-generations indicator } \mathbf{F_k}. \end{cases} \quad (9\text{-}31)$$

$\mathbf{F_k(A)}$ reflects the future-generations value of economic arrangement $\mathbf{A}$ regarding indicator $\mathbf{F_k}$.

The following vector represents the future-generations value of economic arrangement $\mathbf{A}$ regarding future-generations indicators $\mathbf{F_i,...,F_k,...,F_n}$.

$$\mathbf{F(A) = [F_1(A),...,F_k(A),...,F_p(A)]} \quad (9.32)$$

To get an aggregate picture of the future-generations value of economic arrangement A we should introduce weights that reflect the relative importance of indicators $\mathbf{F_1,...,F_k,...,F_p}$. Let $\mathbf{v_i,...,v_k,...,v_p}$ be such importance weights.

It is required that

$$\sum v_k = 1 \tag{9.33}$$

The aggregate future-generations value of economic arrangement A can be calculated as follows:

$$\sum v_k F_k(A) \tag{9.34}$$

F(A) reflects the aggregate future-generations value of economic arrangement **A**

$$(1 \geq F(A) \geq -2).$$

The forms of (9.29) and (9.33) assure that aggregate social value and aggregate future-generations value of economic arrangement A are comparable.

A balance between society and future generations is established if

$$C(A) \approx F(A) \tag{9.35}$$

This means that the economic arrangement produces approximately equal values for society and future generations.

If (9.35) is held then it implies that future generations are not discounted at all. Present generations and future generations are different in their ontological status. Present generations have positively defined real interests while future generations have negatively defined hypothetical interests. For this reason reconciling the interests of present and future generations is not hopeless, as the experiences of American aboriginal societies show.

The biblical adage admonishes to "love your neighbor as yourself." This can be applied to nature, society and future generations, too. It is realized if the following triple of equality is held:

$$E(A) \approx C(A) \approx F(A) \tag{9.36}$$

The underlying principle of justice among nature, society, and future generations can be read as follows: "Love Nature and Future Generations as your own Society."

9.7 Summary

John Rawls argues that in the "original position," people rationally choose his conception of justice. It can be shown that responsible persons would accept the difference principle in the "actual position," where each of them knows perfectly well her or his own position in society. Average, above-average and below average persons would accept the difference principle if they equally considered the deontological, the goal-achievement and the stakeholder values of accepting such a principle of justice.

The Paradox of a Paretian Liberal reveals that normative social policy cannot be based on individual preferences alone. The information provided by individual preferences might not be sufficient to make an accurate social ordering over the states of affairs. Deontological considerations and stakeholder considerations should also be used in social evaluation to get a more accurate picture of the states of affairs.

The standard solution to the prisoner's dilemma game is based on the self-interest of the players. In reality people do not always maximize their self-interests as prescribed by standard game theory. People tend to cooperate in prisoner's dilemma situations in many real world cases. In light of the responsible decision making model, the possible strategies in the prisoner's dilemma game can be reevaluated. Both the cooperative strategy and the noncooperative strategy can be evaluated from deontological, goal-achievement, and stakeholder perspectives. When applying the maximin rule, the cooperative strategy pays better than the noncooperative strategy does. Responsible agency can lead to optimal outcomes in prisoner's dilemma situations. What rational, self-interested players are not able to reach can be realized by responsible agents.

The underlying idea of cost-benefit analyses is that a project is worthy of being undertaken if and only if the state of affairs with the project is better than the state of affairs without the project. The responsible decision making model suggests that a project should be undertaken if the state of affairs with the project is better than the state of affairs without the project when considering environmental, monetary, and social values simultaneously. The irreducible complexity of resource allocation can be handled with the help of the maximin rule, which permits only limited tradeoffs among different values. Quality of life can be preserved and enhanced if decision makers pay equal attention to all the relevant value perspectives in the decision situation.

The ethical performance of a business organization can be determined by evaluating its activities from the perspective of the applying ethical norms. The social performance of a business organization can be determined by evaluating its impacts on the stakeholders. Profit-generating activities of a business organization are acceptable if they do not violate the relevant ethical norms and cause no harm to the stakeholders. Hence nonviolence emerges as a necessary and sufficient condition for the ethical and social acceptability of profit making.

Any economic arrangement affects nature, society and future generations. An economic arrangement is hardly legitimate if it produces negative payoffs for these primordial stakeholders. Justice among nature, society and future generations is established if the economic arrangement produces approximately equal values for nature, society and future generations. This may lead to an extension of the biblical adage to the form, "Love Nature and Future Generations as your own Society."

10. Epilogue: The Responsible Person

The responsible person is characterized by having an ability to assume multiple perspectives and make optimal balances across diverse value dimensions. Sociology and developmental psychology can help us finding some basic character traits of the responsible person.

Amitai Etzioni describes the "properly socialized person" as one who represents a middle way between the Tory view of an oversocialized person and the Whig view of an undersocialized person (Etzioni, A. 1988: pp. 13-14).

The undersocialization view is closely linked to the Enlightenment notion, which is very sanguine about the individual ability to reason. It assumes that people set their own goals and the ways they pursue their goals. The person may err in her or his decisions, but when exposed to valid norms for logical, scientific, and statistical thinking will acknowledge the errors and seek to reform the faulty practice (Shweder, R. 1986). This assumption is at the core of mainstream economics.

The oversocialization view is linked to what has been called the romantic worldview, which holds that the foundation of knowledge is provided by the particular culture to which a person belongs. According to this viewpoint, all facts and logical conclusions are evident merely to those who share a cultural paradigm. Not only is what is held to be true defined by the paradigm of a culture, but also the criteria by which statements are validated, which are strictly subjective or integral to one's paradigm (Shweder, R. 1986).

The idea of a properly socialized person suggests that the goals people pursue are not universal or stable over time but instead fluctuate and vary greatly, and they cannot be arranged into a neat, overarching monolithic scheme. People are members of divergent social collectivities. Hence there is a dynamic of forces that determine a person's socialization, as well as her or his deviation or rebellion against a prescribed set of goals (Etzioni, A. 1988: p. 14).

The responsible person is certainly a properly socialized individual who has developed reflexivity with the ethical norms of a given society and displays empathy toward the others with whom a common environment is shared.

The attachment theory developed by psychologists John Bowly, M.D.S. Ainsworth and others gives some meaningful insights into the basic formation of a person (Bowly, J. 1969; Ainsworth, M.D.S. et al 1978; Main, M.; Kaplan, N. and Cassidy, J. 1985; van Uzendorn, M. H. and Zwart-Woudstra, H.A. 1995).

The central thesis of the attachment theory is that children construct complex internal working models of the world and the significant persons in it, including the self. The working models are considered representations of attachment patterns that influence the children's interpretations of and expectations about the caregiver's behavior toward them, and which guide their own behavior in attachment relationships.

Psychological studies of adolescents and adults show that the internal working models of attachment continue to exist throughout the entire life span and remain relatively stable over time.

Individuals are classified as dismissing, secure-autonomous, or preoccupied based on their attachment patterns. A dismissing person displays strong materialistic orientation, independence and limited ability to take the perspective of others. A preoccupied person is over-dependent on others, has little self-esteem and displays depression in problematic situations. Only a secure-autonomous person manifests a strong sense of self, exercises a balanced strategy, and displays sensitivity to the signals of others.

Autonomous attachment may be at the core of mature moral reasoning. As a recent empirical study concluded, "only individuals with a strong personal identity and a balanced perspective on their personal (attachment) history may have the ability to internalize the ideals of mature morality and to act accordingly. If they fail to live up to their ethical ideals, their self-definition may be at stake" (van Uzendorn, M. H. and Zwart-Woudstra, H.A. 1995: p. 370).

The components of the 3R model of responsibility, namely reverence for the ethical norms, rationality in goal-achievement, and respect for others can be considered virtues. These are motivational dispositions that determine ways individuals tend to act in certain sorts of circumstances.

One might ask if taking responsibility is a virtue, too. It is, but of a different kind. We described responsibility as a synthesis of reverence, rationality, and respect. So responsibility is about how to act with other (first-order) virtues. For this reason taking responsibility can be considered a second-order virtue.

Harry G. Frankfurt made an important distinction between the first-order desires and the second-order will of the person (Frankfurt, H.G. 1988). The wholehearted will of responsibility is what constitutes the responsible person.

Appendix

I. Implementing Environmental Principles*

In this study the most important environmental principles are analyzed, those that play an important role in implementing environmental policies in the EU and other countries of the world. These principles are as follows: the precautionary principle; the "polluter pays" principle; the principle of prevention; the principle of correction at source; the sustainable development principle; and the subsidiarity principle.

We reconstructed the history and the interpretations of the principles in the context of the European Union. The environmental principles under study do not form a coherent system. It is better to consider them as historically developed and co-evolved ideas that can provide value background for environmental policies. To provide some comparative reference, we studied the implementation of environmental principles in Germany, Portugal and Hungary.

---

* This paper is based on the results of the project *Comparative Survey between the European Union and Hungary Focusing on the Implementation of Environmental Principles,* which was carried out at the Hungarian Prime Minister's Office from September 1999 through February 2000. The project was financially supported by the PHARE program of the European Union. The final report was produced by the project leader, Laszlo Zsolnai. Part 1, "Understanding Environmental Principles," is based on the papers provided by Gyorgy Pataki, Zsolt Boda and Zsuzsanna Patho. Part 2, "The German Experience," is based on the report "Implementation of EU environmental principles in Germany" produced by Hauke von Seht and Dr. Hermann Ott of the Wuppertal Institute. Chapter 3, "The Portugal Experience," is based on the paper "Implementation of Environmental Principles in Portugal" written by Dr. Rocha Janudrio of SNEDE, SA Lisbon. Finally, Chapter 4, "Environmental principles in Hungary," is based on the contributions by Gyorgy Pataki, Zsolt Boda and Zsuzsanna Patho. Throughout the realization of the project we received continuous support from Janos Vargha, senior advisor in Environmental Affairs, Prime Minister's Office, Hungary.

1. Understanding Environmental Principles

(I) The precautionary principle

The adoption of the precautionary principle is a response to the recognition of scientific uncertainty in environmental management. The underlying rationale of the precautionary principle originates from a legal concept in German national law called "Vorsorgeprinzip." "Vorsorge," as it appeared in 1971 in the German Federal Government environmental program, meant state-influenced planning and the removal of economic efficiency criteria from policies demanding more than damage repair.

Since the late 1980s, the precautionary principle has been referred to in numerous national environmental management strategies and international agreements, in relation to a range of environmental issues. Among the numerous international agreements, the 1992 Rio Declaration on Environment and Development was the most significant recognition of the principle.

The precautionary principle has a core meaning. There are three elements common to all interpretations: (i) regulatory inaction threatens nonnegligible harm; (ii) there exists a lack of scientific certainty on the cause-and-effect relationship; and (iii) under these circumstances, regulatory inaction is unjustified.

The innovative characteristic of the precautionary principle is that it does not require scientific proof about the cause-effect relationship, whereas the preventive approach implies the duty of due diligence only when the negative environmental outcome is inevitable. The essence of precaution is that once risk is identified, scientific uncertainty should not be used as a reason to postpone or neglect protective actions.

The precautionary principle has moved from being a general guiding principle to one that will hopefully establish its position in an international setting as a rule of law guiding the behavior of decision makers.

Article 130r(2) of the Treaty of EU provides a general guideline for policy. All actions must be taken by virtue of this article, but the directly binding nature of the principles articulated is debatable. Alongside the preventive action principle, the principle of rectification at source, the polluter pays principle and the subsidiarity principle, the precautionary principle is part of the European treaty law. Aside from being part of

European treaty law, the Union and its member states have a binding obligation to adhere to the principle by signing various international environmental agreements. Regarding case law, the European Union has already used this principle for defending its position in disputes. The principle appears in the environmental *acquis communautaire* of the European Union as well.

The principle was transposed from the international scene to the new framework law on the environment in 1995. The law defines precaution as "decision or measure necessary to prevent or minimize the environmental risk and future environmental damage." Further on it refers explicitly to the precautionary principle as fundamental to environmental protection.

The National Environmental Strategy of Hungary—which is, together with the framework law, the basis for all actions in the field of the environment—devoted a paragraph to the principle. In addition to its national laws, Hungary, like the EU, is a signatory to several international treaties invoking the precautionary principle.

(II) The "polluter pays" principle

The polluter pays principle (PPP) is one of the most important guidelines for environmental policy. It was approved by the European Council in the first Environmental Action Programme in 1973.

The European Communities Single European Act (SEA) 1987 has actually incorporated the polluter pays principle into general environmental policy by adding Title VII to the Treaty, which defines community principles of action in the field of environmental protection. As amended by the Treaty of Maastricht 1992, community environmental action is founded on the principle, among others, that the "polluter pays."

The recommendation of 1975 adopted by the EU Council attempts to define the methods of the application of PPP. In defining the perpetrator it states that "a polluter is someone who directly or indirectly damages the environment or who creates conditions leading to such damage." As a further specification, it states that polluters can be "natural or legal persons governed by public or private law."

As to the questions of what and how much a polluter should pay, the Council recommendation of 1975 first states that those "who are responsible for pollution must pay the costs of such measures as are necessary to eliminate that pollution or to reduce it"; and, "environmental protection should not in principle depend on policies which rely on grants of aid and place the burden of combating pollution on the community." As the Council recommendation of 1975 explains, the "costs to be borne by the polluter should include all the expenditure necessary to achieve an environmental quality objective, including the administrative costs directly linked to the implementation of anti-pollution measures" (but probably excluding monitoring and supervisions-related costs). This interpretation of costs was further strengthened and clarified by the European Court of Justice in a 1998 opinion and 1999 judgment stating that PPP "must be understood as requiring the person who causes the pollution, and that person alone, to bear not only the costs of remedying the pollution, but also those arising from the implementation of a policy of prevention."

PPP's compatibility with certain kinds of public grants or aids is the most hotly debated question in practice. It was referred to above as "the political economy of PPP," and some authors even state that PPP has been reinterpreted along national interests.

In the first environmental action program the possibility was granted for exceptions under PPP. The Council recommendation of 1975 also attempted to clarify it. Accordingly, exceptions are justified in limited cases: (i) where its application is "likely to lead to serious economic disturbances," there may be a justified time allowance for adapting and/or granting aid for a limited period; (ii) "where in the context of other policies (...), investment affecting environmental protection benefit from aid intended to solve certain industrial, agricultural or regional structural problems."

Though the Council recommendation of 1975 argued that three categories of financing shall not be viewed contrary to PPP—(i) financial contributions granted to local authorities for public installations if revenues from charges levied on polluters cannot cover the full costs; (ii) compensation for particularly heavy costs; and (iii) contributions to environmental research-and-development activities—it is by no means clear in what concrete circumstances aid granted to clean technological improvements under (ii) should be allowed and applied. In this respect, Council Regulation No. 1973/92 of 21 May 1992, establishing a financial instrument for the environment (LIFE), may provide some further guidance.

(III) The principle of prevention

The principle of prevention is certainly one of the most fundamental principles of environmental policy. Its meaning in a broader sense lies at the very core of any environmental protection measure: preventing the impairment or damage from occurring and reducing the harmful effects to the natural environment.

In this general sense, prevention might be considered almost synonymous with environmental protection, complementing the two other general goals of environmental policy: conservation (preserving and safeguarding ecosystems and natural resources) and improvement (restoring the natural and human environment, cleaning up pollution and repairing damage).

The concept of prevention has also a more restricted and more technical use, referring specifically to pollution prevention and waste minimization. Often in this more technical usage, well-formulated definitions specify what kinds of pollution and waste minimization are to be considered as "preventive actions." In such cases, these definitions obviously fulfill administrative functions. The EU adopted the more general use of the principle, while in most of the international or US environmental policy documents, this technical meaning is given priority.

While many international treaties do not build explicitly on the principle of prevention, it is one of the declared principles of action in the European Community's environmental policy. The first program of the Community Environmental Policy, adopted on 22 November 1973, accords special attention to the principle of prevention.

Prevention is the first of the 11 principles elaborated in the Action Programmes: "1. The best environmental policy consists in preventing the creation of pollution and nuisance at source, rather than subsequently trying to counteract their effects."

The "technical" uses of the concept of prevention generally seek to restrict its meaning to certain measures while excluding others with the clear aim of identifying those measures which are "more preventive" (that is, more valuable) than others. The three principles of waste management, for instance, differentiate between "the prevention of generating waste," "recycling" and "safe disposal." In a general sense, however, even "safe disposal" might be considered a preventive measure when compared to uncontrolled disposal of waste.

These technical uses of the concept of prevention do certainly fulfill administrative and legal functions and can serve as a basis for environmental policy measures. For instance, they can contribute to defining the "best available technologies" and serve as a basis for preferential treatment (e.g., credits or voluntary agreements), etc. There is, however, a question as to whether the principle of prevention in its general formulation has any legal status.

But even if the principle does not apply to each individual action, it certainly "requires each Party to exercise 'due diligence,' i.e., to act reasonably and in good faith and to regulate public and private activities subject to its jurisdiction or control that are potentially harmful to any part of the environment. The principle does not include a minimum threshold of harm, because obligation is one of conduct (due diligence), not of result."

Two basic documents inform and direct policy measures in the environmental field in Hungary: the framework law on the environment and the National Environmental Programme.

The prevention principle appears in both of the two documents, together with the principles of "sustainable development," "precaution," "partnership" and "stewardship." The prevention principle is given four paragraphs in the National Environmental Programme; its meaning is close to the general sense of the principle embraced by EU documents. Prevention is related to sustainable development and is justified both on economic (preventive measures are less costly than repairing damage) and ecological (irreversible losses should be prevented) grounds.

Putting the principles into practice requires the following "musts": "environmental protection inform technological development"; "environmentally friendly products be widespread"; "environmentally harmful materials be substituted"; "any innovation be supported which leads to reducing the load on the environment"; and even, "indirect environmental protection measures be supported."

The idea of prevention lies at the very core of any environmental protection policy. Despite (or specifically because of) this fact, the principle is not formulated explicitly in the most important international environmental treaties. Or if it is, its meaning is rather restricted to the concept of "pollution prevention." Thus it seems that apart from the technical meanings of pollution prevention, when definitions seek to establish the difference between "more preventive" (that is, more valuable) and "less preventive" environmental measures, the principle has a rather minor role in environmental law.

(IV) The principle of correction at source

The idea that pollution should be rectified at source is the weakest formulation of the proactive approach to environmental damage. The "rectification at source" —> "prevention" —> "precaution" line means a gradual shift to wards an acknowledgement of the ineffectiveness of the traditional pollute-clean up approach.

The principle of rectification at source has widely differing interpretations. Its weakest interpretation requires that pollution be dealt with where and when it has occurred. In this sense it is still a reactive policy. Another possible interpretation is that pollution should be minimized at the source, thus preventing a certain amount of the pollution. This would amount to a partially preventive approach, which can be explained by cost or political feasibility considerations. Another possible meaning of the principle is simply prevention that calls for measures to be taken to prevent the impairment or damage from occurring.

The commonly used meaning of the principle is that pollution should be dealt with at the source. This definition recognizes that the previous practice of shifting the pollution from one environmental medium to another is hypocritical. The principle of rectification at source is a tentative answer to the regulatory problem arising from the definition of boundaries. Environmental law is organized around environmental media (air, water, soil, ecosystems, etc.), thus a shift of pollution means, in the regulatory sense, a change in the applicable piece of law. Tracing back to the "original" polluter is usually a huge burden—both financially and administratively—to the state. The cost of rectification increases with time and the distance pollution travels, as the impairment tends to expand as it moves farther from its source.

Placing the requirement of the principle in an international context, it clearly addresses equity issues. Exporting environmental damage to developing countries, for example, has a long history. The best example is probably the export of hazardous waste, which has already attracted attention in international politics as well.

The principle is often cited in EU documents. It was inserted into the Treaty in 1987 and invoked in front of the European Court of Justice as well. The Court has justified a regional import ban on waste on the basis of this and other principles and stated that waste should be disposed as close to the place of its generation as possible. As far as the emissions versus ambient-quality standard is concerned, the EU has a tendency to favor the latter in the name of deregulation and flexibility. Hence the EU is not following this interpretation of the principle in its policymaking.

(V) The principle of sustainable development

The notion of sustainable development was popularized by the 1987 report of the Brundtland Commission. Since then literature has amassed exploring the idea and undeniable political success has resulted. It has become an obligatory term of reference for national environmental policies and most of the important international economic organizations (WTO, EU, OECD) have also embraced it as a general policy objective.

The following represents the short definition of the concept: "Sustainable development is development that meets the needs of the present without compromising the ability of future generations to meet their own needs."

The Brundtland Commission formulated and defined sustainable development in a way that would avoid too much emphasis on international equity issues (addressed by the New International Economic Order document), binding ecological constraints (highlighted by the "limits to growth" approach) or local needs (stressed by the concept of ecodevelopment). Sustainable development does not entail cutting growth; neither does sustainable development entail restructuring or reducing international trade. This is reflected in the text of Agenda 21 and in the Rio Declaration.

Apart from the politically dominant interpretation of sustainable development, many other interpretations exist. As it is sometimes noted, it is not a lack of consensus on its meaning but rather the practical implications of achieving sustainable development that are responsible for the diversity of approaches. It is unclear what the condition would be for not impairing the ability of future generations to meet their needs, and different approaches have been worked out to operationalize this condition.

Although the European Parliament, in its 1992 resolution on a Community program of policy regarding sustainable development, expressed its wish that agreement be reached on a comprehensible and precise definition of what is meant by the term, the European Community Programme launched in 1993 adopted the Brundtland Commission's definition.

That sustainable development is a general policy objective without a precise role, content or implications is substantiated by the way the concept is introduced into the EU by the 1997 Amsterdam Treaty. The Preamble to the Treaty mentions that economic and social progress shall take sustainable development into account and promote it in the context of environmental protection. Sustainable development also appears among the "tasks" in Article 2; however, it is related to economic growth.

Sustainable development is among the general objectives of the EU. There is the possibility, however, that sustainable development is in conflict with other objectives. As no hierarchy exists between the objectives of the EU, each of them shall be attained. Should individual objectives conflict, the EU institutions must find a compromise.

Sustainable development appears among the "principles" of Hungarian environmental policy. In the National Environmental Program it is defined as follows:

> Sustainable development is meant to implement two aspects which are not considered by the market, that of the preservation of environmental values and the principle of responsibility towards future generations. The environmental dimension of the sustainable development of the society means the sustainable use of the environment, that is, the principle is that the quality of human life shall be improved while the limits of the carrying and regenerative capacities of life supporting ecological systems shall be respected. Sustainable development assumes that equilibrium can be attained between the aim of meeting needs and preserving environmental values. The key point is the need of preserving the elements of life (water, soil, air) and the nature. Implementing the principle requires the use of a range of non-market mechanisms. The principle shall be implemented on local, regional and global levels.

This principle is the first among the environmental principles, and it seems that the others are somehow subsumed under the umbrella of sustainable development. However, sustainable development is not operationalized in Hungary, either.

(VI) The principle of subsidiarity

Subsidiarity was spelled out reasonably clearly for the first time in the Single European Act (SEA) of 1987, where the chapter on environmental policy states, "The Community shall take action relating to the environment to the extent to which the objectives referred to in paragraph 1 can be attained better at Community level than at the level of the individual Member States."

The Maastricht Treaty is widely considered to be a major turning point with regard to the principle of subsidiarity. The Treaty formally introduced it "as a general principle into EC and EU law," symbolizing and contributing to "a gradual change in the political and legal culture of the EC" from a "self-conscious teleology of integration" to a "teleology of subsidiarity."

The broader, political concept of subsidiarity encompasses not only a view of intra-state relations but a view of the proper relationship between state and society as well. Politically it relates to three current European ideologies, namely the Christian democratic ideology, German federalism and British conservatism.

Turning to the other leading interpretation of subsidiarity, with its "narrower," "legal" or "procedural" sense, it may be useful to point out that three preconditions must be satisfied under Article 3b of the Maastricht Treaty: "the area concerned must not fall within the Community's exclusive competence; the objectives of the proposed action cannot be sufficiently achieved by Member States; the action can therefore, by reason of its scale and effects, be implemented more successfully by the Community."

According to the principle of subsidiarity as a procedural criterion,

> the Community should take action [in areas that do not fall within its exclusive competence] only if and in so far as the objectives of the proposed action cannot be sufficiently achieved by the Member States and can therefore, by reason of the scale or effects of the proposed action [the so-called "added value" test], be better achieved by the Community [the so-called comparative efficiency test]. Any action by the Community shall not go beyond what is necessary to achieve the objectives of the Treaty [principle of proportionality].

Thus, subsidiarity, as the principle for determining the appropriate level of policy intervention and guiding policy implementation, consists of a test of "comparative efficiency" and "added value" and is, or rather should be, in harmony with the principle of proportionality. In this respect, the principle of subsidiarity might be hard to differentiate from the basic efficiency criterion in economics.

The principle of subsidiarity is also manifested in the Hungarian Act on Local Governments. However, though there is an acknowledged shared competence between the central and local levels, the high degree of financial dependence of local environmental initiatives on central funding and support can weaken the actual significance and substance of the principle of subsidiarity.

2. The German Experience

Germany has often been called a European leader on environmental issues. This certainly was partially true in the past. Germany introduced ambitious environmental protection legislation earlier than other EU Member States, and for some time, Germany also pushed EU environmental policy.

Regarding environmental principles in particular it can be added that, for example, the idea of precaution even evolved out of the German sociolegal tradition (and is still very important for German environmental policy). Furthermore, the new official EU principle of subsidiarity has been one of the cornerstones of the postwar German political system since its beginning.

Germany has a wealth of experience with environmental principles. There are good examples as well as possible sticking points. However, even though all environmental principles of the EU have been implemented to some extent in Germany, they have not been implemented in full and in all fields.

As an example, Germany recently introduced new energy taxes, taking into account, inter alia, the polluter pays principle, but the taxes do not cover the external cost of energy use. Furthermore, the principle of sustainable development has not been implemented in a persuasive way. Among other things, there is no general principle that materials have to be used economically.

In the past, German environmental protection efforts and the implementation of environmental principles were motivated by a range of factors. Certainly the relatively high environmental awareness of German citizens was always important. Furthermore, a few special incidents—such as Chernobyl, the news about forest degradation, ozone depletion and the threat of global warming—have also had a decisive impact in fostering public awareness. And finally, the Green Keynesianism of the 1980s that aimed at opportunities for growth and employment has to be mentioned.

Today, there is still a relatively high level of environmental awareness, but since the recession at the beginning of the 1990s and criticism regarding the impact of environmental protection requirements on competitiveness, environmental progress is hard to achieve, let alone "strong" sustainable development. For large parts of the population, other issues seem more pressing than, for example, the implementation of environmental principles. Furthermore, the costs of the reunification are limiting the financial resources the government has available for environmental protection. Under the new coalition government of the Social Democrats and the Green Party, the conditions for an ambitious environmental policy at the national and international levels did not improve very much.

Following these circumstances, two important goals can be identified in German environmental policy, apart from the aim of protecting the environment. First, that environmental protection efforts shall be facilitated in a way that keeps the costs for the state low. A major means for achieving this is the more rigorous application of the polluter-pays principle. Examples are the charges for the abstraction of drinking water, which have recently been introduced, and the new energy taxes. In addition, the Power Feed-in Act can be seen in line with this aim, because it does not require the state to pay for the related costs of supporting renewable energies. The second aim is to ensure that the measures chosen do not harm the economy, or at least are not perceived as harmful. In the best case, they should rather bring about economic gains.

One problem is the tendency to base environmental policy to a larger extent on voluntary commitments of businesses rather than formal laws. Certainly it is sensible to implement the principle of cooperation by consulting all the affected or interested groups before adopting a law. Among other things, this improves the information base. Voluntary commitments, however, may often lead to weak results for the environment, due to the strong negotiating position it gives to businesses. It also allows for free riding of whole business sectors, whereby businesses from the relevant sectors fail to accept or implement commitments. Furthermore, democratic principles require taking all interests into account, and voluntary commitments might lead to an overly dominant positioning of business interests.

Another example is again the energy taxes. Members of the government and the ruling political parties presented these taxes to the electorate and business interests as taxes that bring about economic gains, often even omitting reference to their beneficial effects on the environment. According to the main argument used, the revenue recycling included in the concept would help to create or save jobs, while on average avoiding higher costs for businesses. Others held that less money for energy imports would get lost to the economy and measures to restructure the energy sector would provide business opportunities.

Although the economic impacts of certain environmental protection measures are often subject to some controversy, the thesis that energy taxes bring about economic benefits coincides with the general scientific findings on many environmental protection measures. In Germany, past experience shows that environmental protection, if designed effectively, will lead to substantial positive economic impacts. Germany and the US are the world leaders in the market of environmental protection technologies.

It can be stated that the aim of avoiding economic damage does not necessarily entail a major negative impact on German environmental policy and the implementation of environmental principles. If the public can be persuaded of the economic benefits, the prospects for environmental protection are not bad. If economically successful measures are chosen, this might even enhance support for future environmental protection efforts. This will require a move further away from end-of-pipe solutions and foster an input-oriented approach "at source."

In cases where environmental protection measures are perceived as economically harmful, much depends on the overall condition of the economy. If high unemployment prevails, the chances of getting sufficient backing for such environmental protection efforts is limited.

However, it should not be forgotten that there will always be cases where measures have to be taken that are not economically beneficial; for example, when avoiding risks to human life by implementing the precautionary principle. A responsible environmental policy can therefore never be limited to measures that result in economic benefits.

3. The Portugal Experience

In Portugal, environmental principles in the energy sector are mainly realized by the promotion of renewable energy, rational utilization of energy, conservation and diversification of sources.

Since 1988, Portugal has rejected the adoption of nuclear energy. A legal and financial framework was created to stimulate the promotion of renewable energies and co-generation. In spite of the implementation—mainly after 1988—of incentive systems for the promotion of renewable energies, and conservation and rational utilization of the energy, Portugal has yet to develop a fiscal system to stimulate and guide citizens in the field of energy.

Information and sensitizing campaigns on the real value of natural resources for the production and preservation of energy, as well as the need for conservation and rational utilization, are still deficient for both economic agents and citizens in general.

At the energy production level—mainly based on hydro and thermal energy (coal)—there are some fiscal incentives aiming at the preferential utilization of raw materials and combustibles less offensive to the environment; for example, low-sulfur coal.

The management of the large energy producers has been systematically guided by the offer conditions; namely, the final energy low selling price to the consumers (domestic or similar, agricultural and industrial), which does not correspond to a "real price" policy. As already mentioned, the real price expresses the real value of the natural resources utilized for production.

On the other hand, the exploration of markets on the "demand" side is still insignificant in terms of management. This must be done to increase the utilization of technologies and equipment and to promote attitudes and behaviors tending towards the reduction of consumption and the rational utilization of energy.

Structured campaigns of information, sensitization and training on the rational utilization of water are at present almost nonexistent in Portugal. Usually, the grantee entities are legally entrusted with the promotion of the public water supply, sanitation and wastewater treatment by transference of attributions and competencies that in the past belonged to the municipalities.

Not until 1990 did Portugal clearly and definitively establish the legal obligation that "water utilization" should always imply the conservation of this natural resource in acceptable conditions for further reutilization within the concept of preserving and conserving the environment.

Besides being a production factor, water is viewed as a structuring resource for national development, and its management has been oriented within a perspective of economic rationality.

The "water utilization" concept is wider than before. It now covers water as a recipient of effluent discharge and dispersed pollution.

Portuguese law foresees—and allows—the signing of "environmental promotion contracts" between associations representing various sectors of activity and the Ministries of Environment. This is aimed at promoting improved water quality and protecting the environment by means of a progressive reduction of pollution from wastewater discharge into the aquatic environment and soil. These contracts must follow the EU rules, the hydro resources national plans and the action and management plans approved by law. As regards industrial and agro-food plants, these contracts are called "environmental adaptation contracts" and follow a similar regimen.

To rationally promote hydro resources planning and management, Portugal decided in 1990 to establish the following management-units typology within the water utilization concept: The Hydrographic Basin, Groups of Hydrographic Basins, Similar Zones.

Several water resource administrations have also been established at the regional level. These are chaired at technical and financial levels by the Water National Institute, which is responsible for the hydro resources national policy (integrated planning and management).

According to the law, the local autarchies have their own competencies as regards the public supply (including water), basic sanitation and environmental protection in general. They are also entrusted with the promotion of campaigns for sensitizing and informing on the rational utilization of water.

The users of collective undertakings of unique finality (vs. water supply) or multiple finalities (vs. water supply, irrigation and electric energy production) can form associations aiming at the exploration and conservation of those undertakings.

Within this scope, they can operate either directly or through contracts with providers of the specified services. In general, these associations have preference in the attribution of licensing for the utilization of the public hydro resources and for the signature of contract programs (with the state or other public entities) to obtain technical or financial support. The state's financing can be provided by direct participation in the initial investment or by supporting the contracting loans.

In Portugal, water management policy is based on the concept of "public water resource utilization," which includes any act or activity that might cause quantitative or qualitative changes in the water, riverbeds or margins. This would include catchment or deviation of water, retention or low water level, rejection of effluents or the addition of substances, extraction of inerts as well as any occupation of space within the hydro area, no matter which will be the finality.

The utilization of all public hydro resources is subject to authorization (licensing). General purposes for any type of licensing for the utilization of the public hydro resources are as follows: abstain from the practice of acts or activities that might give origin to exhaustion or degradation of the hydro resources or have other environmental impacts; abstain from the practice of acts or activities that might give origin to the nonviability of alternative utilizations that have priority; in terms of the planning guidelines, noncontradiction of the respective basin or hydrographic region.

The beneficiaries of the hydraulic or basic sanitation infrastructures are subject to the payment of exploration, conservation and improvement taxation that will provide revenue for the infrastructure managers and for the funding entities. For the latter purpose, the law establishes the criteria for the sharing of benefits/revenues.

The beneficiaries of the works for the superficial or underground waters regulation, totally or partially carried out by the state, are subject to the payment of a "regulation tax" to compensate both the investment and the exploration and conservation costs.

Those who do not meet the rules applied to the public hydro resources management and exploration are responsible for restoration of the previous conditions. Should restoration be impossible, they will indemnify the state accordingly.

Portugal adopted the concept "cycle of the water utilization," and from it, the minimum levels of water quality were established in accordance with the types of utilization. This resulted in the creation of "environmental quality objectives" (limit-values). Over these limits, the risks to health or the environment are deemed unacceptable.

4. Environmental Principles in Hungary

In this Section the successes and failures of implementing environmental principles in Hungary will be analyzed.

The polluter pays principle, or the principle of internalization of external costs, does appear in the Hungarian energy policy setting. However, while energy legislation and energy policy documents do mention it as an important element of the principle of sustainable development, energy policy programs reflect it very poorly. Hungarian energy policy programs are applying as their main instruments a variety of subsidies, which are mostly derived from the state budget, foreign aid or grants, and to a lesser extent revenues from taxing or charging pollution.

The institutional structure of Hungarian energy policy is a major factor contributing to this state of affairs, since there is very limited integration at the institutional level between the environment and energy policy. The Ministry of Environment and its institutions play a very narrow and limited role in designing and implementing energy legislation, policy, and programs.

Since the major players of Hungarian energy policy are the Ministry of Economic Affairs and the Hungarian Energy Office, it is not surprising that industrial policy issues, particularly liberalization and competitiveness issues, are overpowering environmental considerations.

Environmental considerations are made in the context of technical problems related to energy conservation and energy efficiency. Though they are both important from an environmental point of view, they do not address the problems associated with the absolute level of energy consumption or the corresponding sources of energy. Therefore, it is obvious that renewable energy resources are not taken seriously enough in Hungarian energy politics.

Despite the promising and progressive rhetoric of the recent major energy policy documents released by the Ministry of Economic Affairs, there is no strategic and practical step taken to internalize all the environmental costs of energy production, transmission, and distribution—even in a gradual fashion.

Therefore, a major achievement for Hungarian energy policy would be the strengthening of environmental interest in terms of its institutional background and programs designed for implementation. Strategically, it would require a plan for comprehensive ecological taxation reform, since energy issues are very sensitive from a social policy point of view; therefore, they need to be handled in a complex fashion.

Though prevention and precaution as fundamental environmental principles do not appear in the legal documents of the energy sector, on the level of programs and institutions the Energy Saving and Energy Efficiency Action Plan can serve as the framework for shifting policy focus from emissions control measures to the prevention of pollution generation by implementing energy saving and energy efficiency measures. The effectiveness of the Action Plan will depend on the available financial resources, which will be determined by the date of the introduction of user charges. Without this additional source, the support provided for some of the tasks listed in the Action Plan will remain on the symbolic level.

The framework law on energy remains a major deficiency in the regulation of the sector. It should be prepared on the basis of acknowledged environmental principles; i.e., the principle of prevention, the precautionary principle, the polluter-pays principle and sustainable development. The contradiction between the law on atomic energy and the precautionary principle should be resolved.

The subsidiarity principle is not mentioned at all in basic energy laws and policy papers, while the concept of sustainable development has only recently appeared in energy policy documents and it is missing from the basic energy laws. A more serious problem is that its definition is vague and its field-specific operationalization is utterly lacking. Those strategic policy documents, which would put the concept into practice, do not exist. Therefore, we simply do not know what a sustainable Hungarian energy policy would look like. In policy documents, the term appears to be used as nothing more than a substitute for "environmental protection," embracing any measure that has the aim of preventing pollution or mitigating environmental harm. An important step would be to work out the conception of a sustainable energy system for Hungary. Even if it could not be implemented directly, it would inform Hungarian energy policy and serve as a guide in the direction of an ideal.

A similar problem arises in connection with water policy: no agreed upon conception of sustainable development exists, at least as an ideal. Given that 95 percent of Hungary's freshwater originates from abroad, any sustainability conception must stress international cooperation in the region. As Hungary lies in a basin, it should be motivated to promote international cooperation: Hungary should be a leading force in developing a regionally sustainable water-policy strategy.

Multiple institutions are in charge of water-related environmental issues. While this is something good and reflects existing patterns of subsidiarity in the context of water-management institutions, the institutional divide causes problems, particularly in connection with water-utilization permits. In the name of a holistic approach, it would probably be best to have the Regional Environmental Inspectorates in charge primarily of water-utilization issues; however, considerable institutional development is needed in these agencies poor in resources.

Subsidiarity is missing from the Hungarian energy policy and energy system. The administration is centralized and the energy system is not organized on regional or local levels. Local governments do not have the capabilities either as owners or as regulating agencies to influence the energy policy or the energy companies; participation and partnership are not distinctive features of the Hungarian energy policy. Focusing more on local energy issues and promoting decentralization of the energy system is an important task.

Implementation is the weakest part of environmental policy in Hungary, and this applies equally to the energy-and-environment issue. As we have shown, the implementation of even the new, stricter air quality standards might become problematic because of the lack of monitoring mechanisms. The First National Energy Saving and Energy Efficiency Programme was also poorly implemented.

The causes of the implementation failure can be grouped into the following major categories:

Lack of political support. Energy efficiency has never been highly valued in the policy agenda. The lack of a consistent political will to promote energy efficiency has certainly contributed to the slow and insufficient implementation. For instance, it took four years to introduce energy-consumption labels on refrigerators.

Institutional problems. There is no sole responsible party in the state administration for co-coordinating energy efficiency measures, although this situation might change with the new efficiency program. No regional agencies exist that would, among other things, provide for local energy efficiency programs or serve as consulting centers, etc. Other institutional problems have plagued the country. (See, for example, the failure to implement new technological standards on building insulation because of a lack of monitoring and sanctioning agencies. The task was relegated to municipalities; however, they were not able to fulfill it.)

Financial difficulties. The first National Energy Saving and Energy Efficiency Programme had no financial backing: When resources were provided, they came from the central budget. A tax on energy was proposed under the new program in order to guarantee the financial basis of the measures; however, it was finally rejected. That is, the new program will also be dependent on budget sources; no self-supporting financial mechanism will be provided. The program repeatedly emphasizes the necessity of using foreign (EU) funds for financing. One promising thing is that if environmental-emissions fees are introduced, a part of this revenue is slated for energy efficiency.

Communication problems within the state administration. The lack of consistency on the strategic level and the problems of integration on the policymaking level are reflected in obvious communication problems within the state administration. Interministerial committees on energy and environmental issues are either nonexistent or conducted on ad hoc basis, as illustrated by the work of the committee of the Energy Saving Credit Programme.

5. Summing Up

In our study, major environmental principles that play an important role in implementing environmental policies in the EU were analyzed. These principles of the Community's environmental policy are the following: the precautionary principle; the "polluter pays" principle; the principle of prevention; the principle of correction at source; the sustainable development principle; and the subsidiarity principle.

We reconstructed the history and the interpretations of the principles, in the context of the European Union, and then provided a short overview of their understanding in Hungary. It has been shown that the environmental principles do not form a coherent system. It is better to consider them as historically developed and co-evolved ideas that can provide value background for developing environmental policies.

To provide some comparative reference, we studied the implementation of environmental principles in Germany, Portugal and Hungary.

Germany has often been called a European leader on environmental issues. This was certainly at least partially true in the past. Germany introduced ambitious environmental protection legislation earlier than other EU/EEC Member States, and for some time Germany also pushed EU environmental policy.

Germany has a wealth of experience with environmental principles, which Hungarian stakeholders can learn from. There are good examples as well as possible sticking points. However, even though all environmental principles of the EU have been implemented to some extent in Germany, they have not been implemented in full and in oilfields.

As an example, Germany's energy taxes take into account the polluter pays principle, but the taxes do not cover the external cost of energy use. Furthermore, the principle of sustainable development has not been implemented in a persuasive way. Among other things, there is no general principle stating that materials have to be used economically.

Today, there still is a relatively high level of environmental awareness, but since the recession at the beginning of the 1990s and criticism regarding the impact of environmental protection requirements on competitiveness, environmental progress has become hard to achieve, with or without "strong" sustainable development. For large parts of the population, other issues seem more pressing than implementing environmental principles. Furthermore, the costs of reunification are limiting governmental financial resources available for environmental protection. Under the new coalition government of the Social Democrats and the Green Party, the conditions for an ambitious environmental policy at the national and international levels has not improved very much.

In cases where environmental protection measures are perceived as economically harmful, much will depend on the overall condition of the economy at the time. If high unemployment prevails, the chances of getting sufficient backing for such environmental protection efforts are limited. However, it should not be forgotten that there will always be cases where measures have to be taken that are not economically beneficial; for example, avoiding risks to human life by implementing the precautionary principle. A responsible environmental policy can never be limited exclusively to measures that result in economic benefits.

In Portugal, environmental principles in the energy sector are mainly realized by promoting renewable energy, rational utilization of energy, and conservation and diversification of sources. Since 1988, Portugal has rejected the adoption of nuclear energy as a source. A legal and financial framework was created to stimulate the promotion of renewable energies and co-generation.

In 1990, Portugal clearly and definitively established the legal obligation that "water utilization" should always imply the conservation of this natural resource in acceptable conditions for further reutilization within the concept of preserving and conserving the environment. The "water utilization" concept is wider than before. It now covers water as a recipient of effluents discharge and dispersed pollution.

Portuguese law foresees—and allows—the signing of "environmental promotion contracts" between associations representing various sectors of activity and the Ministries of Environment. This is aimed at promoting water quality improvement and protecting the aquatic environment by means of a progressive reduction of pollution caused by wastewater discharge in the aquatic environment and soil. These contracts must follow EU rules, the hydro resources national plans and the action and management plans approved by law. As regards industrial and agro-food plants, these contracts are called "environmental adaptation contracts" and follow a similar regimen.

According to the law, the local autarchies have their own competencies as regards the public supply (including water), basic sanitation and environmental protection in general. They are also entrusted with the promotion of campaigns to sensitize and inform on the rational utilization of water.

In Portugal, water management policy is based on the concept of "public water resource utilization," which includes any act or activity that might cause quantitative or qualitative changes in the water, riverbeds or margins, namely catchment or deviation of water, retention or low water level, rejection of effluents or addition of substances, extraction of inerts, as well as any occupation of space within the hydro area, no matter which will be the finality.

Portugal adopted the concept "cycle of the water utilization," and from it, the minimum levels of water quality were established in accordance with the types of utilization. This resulted in the creation of "environmental quality objectives" (limit-values). Over these limits, the risks to health or the environment are deemed unacceptable.

The successes and failures of implementing environmental principles in Hungary were documented and analyzed.

The polluter pays principle does appear in the Hungarian energy policy setting. However, while energy legislation and energy policy documents do mention it as an important element of the principle of sustainable development, energy policy programs reflect it very poorly. The institutional structure of Hungarian energy policy is a major factor contributing to this state of affairs, since there is very limited integration at the institutional level between the environment and energy policy. The Ministry of Environment and its institutions play a very narrow and limited part in designing and implementing energy legislation, policy, and programs.

Since the major players of the Hungarian energy policy are the Ministry of Economic Affairs and the Hungarian Energy Office, it is not surprising that industrial policy issues, particularly liberalization and competitiveness, are dominating over environmental considerations. Despite the promising and progressive rhetoric of major energy policy documents recently released by the Ministry of Economic Affairs, no strategic and practical steps are being taken to internalize all the environmental costs of energy production, transmission, and distribution, even in a gradual fashion.

Therefore, a major improvement in Hungarian energy policy would be the strengthening of environmental interest in terms of its institutional background and programs designed for implementation. Strategically, it would require a plan for comprehensive ecological taxation reform, since energy issues are very sensitive from a social policy point of view; therefore, they need to be handled in a complex fashion.

Though the terms prevention and precaution do not appear in the legal documents of the energy sector, the Energy Saving and Energy Efficiency Action Plan can serve as the framework for shifting policy focus from emissions control measures to the prevention of pollution.

The framework law on energy remains a major deficiency in the regulation of the sector. It should be prepared on the basis of acknowledged environmental principles; i.e., the principle of prevention, the precautionary principle, the polluter-pays principle and sustainable development. The contradiction between the law on atomic energy and the precautionary principle should be resolved.

The subsidiarity principle is not mentioned at all in basic energy laws and policy papers. The concept of sustainable development has only recently appeared in energy policy documents, and it is missing from the basic energy laws. Therefore, we simply do not know what a sustainable Hungarian energy policy would look like. In policy documents the term appears to only substitute for "environmental protection," embracing any measure that has the aim of preventing pollution or mitigating environmental harm. An important step would be to work out the conception of a sustainable energy system for Hungary. Even if it could not be implemented directly, it would inform Hungarian energy policy and serve as a guide toward an ideal.

A similar problem arises in connection with water policy: no agreed upon conception of sustainable development exists, at least as an ideal. Given that 95 percent of Hungary's freshwater originates from abroad, any sustainability conception must stress international cooperation in the region. As Hungary lies in a basin, promoting international cooperation should be a paramount concern: Hungary should be a leading force in developing regional, sustainable water policy strategy.

No institution is formally in charge of dealing with sustainable energy policy, and even energy-related environmental issues as such are not well institutionalized. Energy efficiency and saving issues are dealt with by the Hungarian Energy Office in conjunction with a new inter-ministerial body—the Energy Saving, Energy and Environmental Management Public Interest Company. The Ministry of Economy (which is responsible for energy policy) has no environmental or energy-saving department, while the Ministry of Environment has no department on energy-policy issues. The interministerial Council on Sustainable Development has ceased working. This institutional lacuna should be repaired.

Subsidiarity is missing from the Hungarian energy policy and energy system. The administration is centralized and the energy system is not organized on regional or local levels. Local governments do not have the capabilities either as owners or as regulating agencies to influence the energy policy or the energy companies; participation and partnership are not distinctive features of the Hungarian energy policy. Focusing more on local energy issues, and using the liberalization process of the Hungarian energy market as an opportunity, would help promote the important task of decentralizing the energy system.

The transition to strong sustainable development requires substantial changes in patterns of production and consumption to attain an environmentally regulated market, with heightened local self-sufficiency promoted in the context of global markets. In this stage of development, environmental policy is fully integrated across sectors. Clean technologies and product-life-cycle management schemes are extensively used, and a wide range of sustainability indicators is applied in policy-making.

In the perspective of strong sustainable development, the following policy tasks seem indispensable for Hungary as well as other European and non-European countries.

Sustainable development as a fundamental goal of Hungary should be formulated and included in the Constitution. A unified list of environmental principles with their agreed-upon interpretations should be included in the Environmental Act.

Environmental conflicts are unavoidable, but they should be managed by appropriate institutions, such as the Environmental Committee of the Parliament or the National Environmental Council and other participatory bodies. The horizontal integration of environmental policy into the sectorial policies would increase the conflict- management skills and capacities of the government.

The shaping of horizontally integrated development strategies requires contributions from sectorial administration (i.e., ministries and national authorities) in drafting their own concepts, but the integration should be co-coordinated at a higher level to achieve more than merely the least common denominator.

The polluter-pays principle requires financial guaranties and environmental insurance schemes, based on risk assessment procedures, to cover the costs of possible environmental damages that exceed total capital and maximal profits of companies. Recognizing the openness of the Hungarian economy and Hungary's vulnerability to transboundary pollution, provisions for implementation of the polluter-pays principle should be integrated into bilateral and multilateral environmental, water management, and economic treaties and agreements.

Prevention gives priority to environmentally sound technologies over end-of-pipe solutions and requires the application of the best available production technologies in investments. The principle of prevention should be extended to avoid the cul-de-sac types of development patterns of highly industrialized countries, including those of some member states of the European Union.

Implementation of the precautionary principle increases the probability of positive outcomes for conflicts over the environment in public debates during the decision-making phase of projects, because it creates a more balanced situation between citizens and project proponents who have inadequate resources. Environmental education and free access to environmental data should be provided for all citizens to decrease the dominance of interest groups in environmental conflicts.

Subsidiarity requires adjustment of the administration's structure of the country to the ecological compartment units; i.e., natural ecosystems. Transition toward a system of "eco-regions" presupposes reallocation of financial instruments of governmental and municipal authorities according to their responsibility for environmental protection, conservation and ecological restoration.

Conventional economic indicators should be extended to include a set of environmental indicators that directly reflect ecological conditions and changes in the ecosystems. Such indicators, together with economic and social indicators, could provide a comprehensive picture of the quality of life in the country.

II. Alternative Globalization Strategies*

In this paper we explore alternative strategies for companies engaged in globalization. We argue that if business follows the unhindered "market fundamentalist" type of globalization, it could lose its legitimacy. It is better for globalized business to enter into an open dialogue with the global civil society and try to develop a cooperative strategy.

1. Business Should Abandon "Laissez-faire" Capitalism

Without denying the inherent flaws of capitalism, the current crisis of capitalism stems from malpractice, too. Since the turn of this millennium, "laissez-faire" capitalism has been through two major upheavals, largely of its own making. These are the damage to capitalism wrought by the dot.com era and the exposure of dishonesty in high profile cases such as Enron and WorldCom. In both instances, we saw systemic corruption involving many actors—executives, nonexecutive directors, investment banks and analysts, and accounting firms—commingling nefariously under weak regulation and enforcement. No one likes to spoil a party.

If business uncompromisingly supports laissez-faire capitalism on a global scale, then it might destroy itself. George Soros rightly noted some years ago that laissez-faire capitalism undermines the basic values on which open and democratic societies depend. The instabilities and inequalities of the global capitalist system could feed into nationalistic, ethnic and religious fundamentalism (Soros, G. 1998).

The company is a social institution, and the economy is a part of the whole society. Processes of value creation developed by business should be broad and shared. We are talking about the nature and purposes of firms and economic agents. The short-term approach of creating shareholder value destroys the basis for the long-term success and survival of the company. The main value-drivers for a firm are the intangible assets. Reputation, consensus and legitimacy are crucial

---

* The paper was written by the members of the Business Ethics Inter-faculty Group of the Community of European Management Schools (CEMS) under the direction of Laszlo Zsolnai. Co-authors include Zsolt Boda (Corvinus University of Budapest), Tomasz Dolegowski (Warsaw School of Economics), Knut Ims (Norwegian School of Economics & Business Administration, Bergen), Joseph Lozano (ESADE Business School, Barcelona), Eleanor O 'Higgins (University College Dublin) and Antonio Tencati (Bocconi University Milan). The paper was first published in the *European Business Forum* 2004 Autumn pp. 23-24.

resources for the capability of an organization to continue its activities and operations. The increasing criticism of civil society against the current form of capitalism derives from a lack of consensus between business and society. "If we want to sustain capitalism we have to create a less violent, more caring form of it" (Zsolnai, L. (ed.) 2002. p. 7.).

Capitalism needs business leaders of integrity, who see the firm as a socioeconomic entity with obligations to the society of which it is a part. Without overidealizing, it is interesting to note that social democracies such as Norway, Sweden and Canada, which have embraced less laissez-faire capitalism, consistently have the highest levels of human development relative to GNP per capita on the UN Human Development Index. Incidentally, these countries also have low perceived-corruption levels and their companies are seen as being less apt to use bribery to access business abroad. This could be attributable to their form of capitalism being conceived of as serving the ends of society, rather than the other way around, as happens when capitalism becomes perverted.

Business should further develop its own standards, which would lead toward a sustainable world. International business organizations must embrace those global auditing and reporting schemes that insure the accountability and transparency of corporate operations. Business organizations should also be involved in the development of new and more substantial social and environmental standards. We are convinced that the idea of corporate responsibility under the condition of globalization requires international acceptance of substantial standards concerning labor conditions, human rights at the workplace (including the promotion of labor unions) and ecological conditions of business activities.

Business also has a responsibility in contributing to the further development of global governance institutions. Partnership programs, such as the Global Compact proposed by UN General Secretary Kofi Annan, could provide adequate frameworks for constructive cooperation. Global governance requires new institutions. For instance, the existing institutions are state centered; their focus is not on corporate activities. Although it may seem counterintuitive that business would embrace the idea of a new global institution that would monitor corporate activities, the interest of an enlightened business is the leveling of the playing field. The aim would be to strengthen those institutions that constituted the ethical fabric of the global economy. The interest of responsible business would be to contribute to this development rather than oppose it.

No single actor can tackle the challenges that we confront in our world. It is an interdependent world operating within networks, and responsibilities are increasingly shared. It is not just a matter of seeing what companies do well and what they do poorly in isolation. It is a question of seeing how they contribute to the networks of relations they act within. Globalization can only be tackled from a perspective of co-responsibility. In this respect, we should stop speaking in terms of "company and society" and speak instead about "company in society." The market is always situated in social contexts; society should not be subordinated to the market. In a globalized world, companies become actors jointly responsible for the world that we are building. There can be no globalization without companies, but not all company models are acceptable and viable in a globalized world.

2. Business Could Appeal to Politically and Socially Conscious Consumers

Although socially conscious consumers are sometimes only politically correct trend followers, they might serve as allies for developing alternative globalization strategies for business. Alternative strategies are creative ways of serving the special needs of people through unique, not easily substitutable goods and services while meeting the environmental and social standards of society. Businesses can form partnerships with international nongovernmental organizations (INGOs) to foster innovative responses to environmental, social and cultural conflicts. (Greenpeace, Friends of the Earth, and WWF have already established such partnerships with big businesses.)

There are interesting market opportunities for companies that are able to offer new product systems to fulfill the sustainability-oriented needs of critical consumers/citizens: organic foods, fair trade goods, Social Accountability 8000 standard (SA8000) certification, Eco-labeled products, and so on. These are evident and strong signals that it is possible to combine socially responsible behavior with economic and financial success. A firm that considers its impact on natural, social and human capital has the opportunity to attain sustainable positioning in the market thanks to its true and genuine commitment to sustainability. Innovation and the creative capacity to disrupt old business practices are necessary elements in identifying new conditions and acceptable paths for future corporate development.

Ethically conscious investors constitute another major market force that can serve sustainable business. Funds provided by sustainable banking and ethical investors are constantly increasing. Businesses could rely on these funds in their sustainability projects. But businesses should make the first move: It is for them to prove to ethical consumers and ethical investors that they live up to the high ethical expectations. Trust, the key coordinating mechanism between business and its stakeholders, needs to be rebuilt, and the only way to do it is through the clear commitment of business.

3. Business Has a Responsibility to Powerless Stakeholders

As business considerably affects the lives and futures of powerless stakeholders (the poor, the natural environment, vulnerable communities, future generations), it should take their interests seriously.

According to Donaldson and Preston, if we adopt a normative perspective, "stakeholders are persons or groups with legitimate interests in procedural and/or substantive aspects of corporate activity. Stakeholders are identified by their interests in the corporation, whether the corporation has any corresponding functional interest in them" (Donaldson, T. and L.E. Preston 1995, p. 67). In the new connected and global environment, the conventional distinction between primary and secondary stakeholders is inadequate. If a company does not consider the legitimate interests of minorities, disabled people, local communities, the environment and so on, other players with more power (such as the international nongovernmental organizations) could advocate their positions and force the company to meet their requirements. This capability has been clearly exemplified in recent years by independent, Internet-based media orchestrating boycott campaigns against big companies (for example, Nestle, Danone, Shell, Nike, Microsoft). Companies should overcome the shareholder-value paradigm and adopt a more inclusive stakeholder-value perspective.

Businesses can also contribute positively to powerless stakeholders, because they are engaged with them, whether these stakeholders are employees or host country citizens affected by their operations. Businesses are accountable to these stakeholders, who must be treated fairly and with dignity. Business can apply its financial leverage to influence host country governments to use its revenues appropriately. In this regard, it can work with NGOs. An example is the Publish

What You Pay (PWYP) campaign to require companies to publish all receipts for fuel and mineral exploration and exploitation rights (so called "signature bonus") and franchises. The problem with these initiatives is that, to be effective, they require industry-wide adherence and enforcement. Otherwise, responsible and honest companies could be unfairly penalized.

In the new global context, the company whose only vision of success is measured in financial terms may encounter serious problems of legitimacy in the face of society and public opinion. Many classical themes of business rhetoric (creation of wealth, value and jobs, for example) lose their legitimacy because they are not sufficient any more. The challenge is to go beyond a pragmatic vision of mere reputation management. A complex society makes business legitimacy more complex. Subjects such as the multistakeholder approach or the partnership are just a reflection that people (as citizens and as consumers) expect more than just good products and good services from companies. Companies have to respond to society not just by showing good results, but also by showing their contributions to a more sustainable and equitable world. Issues that were at one time considered irrelevant to business (reducing poverty or promoting human rights, for example) are today on the business agenda. Companies should not assume the form of NGO's or take on governmental functions, but they should consider all the value dimensions affected by their activities.

4. Clean Your Own "Mess"

Business is responsible for cleaning its own "mess." Corporate philanthropy is a nice thing, but it comes after social responsibility. Business should perform its duties to its stakeholders. Although fighting against poverty is not the primary role of business it can contribute to decreasing poverty by playing its main role of providing and distributing goods and services for society. Companies should develop human and social capital in the way they operate. This increases their chance of creating wealth that opens up opportunities for everyone and benefits the poor.

Alternative globalization means that business seeks a better integration into the local communities. "Predator" strategies, when companies look for short-term advantages and a rapid exploitation of local resources (human and natural), can evidently not constitute a basis for sustainable business. Companies, while embracing global ethical standards, should adapt to local social, cultural and ecological circumstances. They should respect and protect local diversities and enhance the well-being of local societies and natural ecosystems. Alternative globalization is also about finding a creative and responsible balance between globalization and localization.

During the World Economic Forum's Annual Meeting in 2004, former US President Bill Clinton called for "systematization" for peace and humane globalization. To face up to the great emergencies of the planet (the HIV/AIDS epidemic, water scarcity, the gap between the rich and the poor, global warming and so on), a systemic approach is needed. In adopting a shared responsibility, public authorities, companies and citizens should collaborate to find solutions for a more equitable form of globalization. The business community has the knowledge and resources to change the world. Thus, responsible companies, at their own levels, should voluntarily contribute through their decisions and actions "to a better society and a cleaner environment" (Commission of the European Communities, 2001, p. 4).

We believe that the business world has a great opportunity in the globalization process. The opportunity does not involve being defensive and purely reactive to criticisms. It is time to develop a true business leadership. The new realities show that a single company model is impossible, and that debate which includes rival visions of company success is required. We should not succumb to the temptation of believing that a globalized world allows only a single-subject discourse on the company. The debate about which subjects should be included in the business agenda (e.g., sustainability, social cohesion, reduction of poverty, partnership, links with the community, social innovation, a commitment to values) is not just a debate about agendas but models and visions as well. And this debate creates a new opportunity for business leadership, insofar as it requires a commitment that has to result in renewing business management. The dialogue and the debate on alternatives to globalization do not have their dividing line between the business world and the nonbusiness world. The dividing line is increasingly internal to the business world itself. The slogan "another world is possible" is not the privilege of politics or of the third sector. This slogan, "another world is possible," could also be a motto for business because another business world is also possible.

Alternative globalization strategies can produce real progress. Companies and their stakeholders can win in a meaningful way. Only those companies, which take the social and environmental challenges of globalization seriously, and are able to develop their strategies creatively and responsibly, will be legitimate and survive into the future.

References

Ackoff, R.L. 1974: *Redesigning the Future.* 1974. New York & London, John Wiley & Sons.

Ainsworth, M.D.S. et al. 1978: *Patterns of Attachment: A Psychological Study of the Strange Situation.* 1978. Hillsdale, NJ, Erlbaum.

Allais, M. 1953: "Le compartement de l'home rationel devant le risque: Critique des postulates et axiomes de l'ecole Americaine" *Econometrica* 1953 October. pp. 503-546.

Anscombe, G.E.M. 1958: "Modern Moral Philosophy" *Philosophy* 1958. No. 1. pp. 1-190.

Azar, C. et al. 1996: "Socio-Ecological Indicators for Sustainability" *Ecological Economics* 1996. pp. 89-112.

Bartee, E.M. 1973: "A Holistic View of Problem Solving" *Management Science* 1973. pp. 439-48.

Bandura, A. et al. 1996: "Mechanisms of Moral Disengagement in the Exercise of Moral Agency" *Journal of Personality and Social Psychology* 1996. No. 2. pp. 364-374.

Bandura, A.; G-V. Caprara and L. Zsolnai 2000: "Corporate Transgression through Moral Disengagement Manuscript" *Journal of Human Values* 2000 No. 1. pp. 57-64.

Bateson, G. 1979: *Mind and Nature: A Necessary Unity.* 1979. New York, Dutton.

Benjamin, M. 1992: "Compromise" in Lawrence Becker & Charlotte B. Becker (eds.): *Encyclopaedia of Ethics.* 1992. New York & London, Garland Publishing, Inc. pp. 189-191.

Bernstein, R.J. 1995: "Rethinking Responsibility" in *The Legacy of Hans Jonas.* Hastings Center Report 1995, No. 7. pp. 13-20. Bowly, J. 1969: *Attachment and Loss.* 1969. New York, Basic Books.

Brown-Weis, E. 1989: *In Fairness to Future Generations: International Law, Common Patrimony, andIntergeneration Equity.* 1989. The United Nations University, Tokyo & Transnational Publishers, Inc. Dobbs Ferry, New York.

Capra, F. 1980: "Buddhist Physics" in Satish Kumar (ed.): *The Schumacher Lectures.* 1980. New York, Harper & Row, Publishers, pp. 121-136.

Capra, F. 1996: *The Web of Life: A New Scientific Understanding of Living Systems.* 1996. New York, Anchor Books, Doubleday.

Cohen, M.D.; J.G. March and J.P. Olsen 1978: "A Garbage Can Model of Organizational-*Choice" Administrative Science Quarterly* 1978. No. 3.

Commission of the European Communities 2001: *Green Paper. Promoting a European-Framework for Corporate Social Responsibility,* Brussels, COM(2001) 366 final.

Conlisk, J. 1996: "Why Bounded Rationality?" *Journal of Economic Literature* 1996 July. pp. 669-700.

Dawes, R. M.; A.J.C. van de Kragt and J.M. Orbell 1990: "Cooperation for the Benefit of Us—Not Me, or My Conscience" in Jane J. Mansbridge (ed.): *Beyond Self-Interest.* 1990. Chicago & London, The University of Chicago Press, pp. 97-110.

Donaldson, T. 1989: *The Ethics of International Business.* 1989. New York, Oxford University Press.

Donaldson, T. and L.E. Preston 1995: "The Stakeholder Theory of the Corporation: Concepts, Evidence, and Implications" *The Academy of Management Review,* Vol. 20, No. 1. pp. 65-91.

Ellsberg, D. 1961: "Risk, Ambiguity, and the Savage Axiom" *Quarterly Journal of Economics* 1961. pp. 643-669.

Elster, J. 1983: *Sour Grapes.* 1983. Cambridge, Cambridge University Press.

Elster, J. 1984: *Ulysses and the Sirens.* 1984. Cambridge, Cambridge University Press.

Elster, J. 1989: *The Cement of Society.* 1989. Cambridge, Cambridge University Press.

Elster, J. 1990: "When Rationality Fails" in Karen Schweers-Cook & Margaret Levi (eds.): *The Limits of Rationality.* 1990. Chicago & London, University of Chicago Press, pp. 19-51.

England, P. and B. Stanek Kilbourne 1990: "Feminist Critiques of the Separative Model *of Self'Rationality and Society* 1990 April, pp. 156-171.

Etzioni,A. 1988: *The Moral Dimension.* 1988. New York, The Free Press.

Etzioni, A. 1992: "Normative-Affective Factors: Toward a New Decision-Making Model" in Mary Zey (ed.): *Decision Making: Alternatives to Rational Choice Models.* 1992. Sage Publications, pp. 89-111.

Ferber, M.A. and J.A. Nelson (eds.) 1993: *Beyond Economic Man.* 1993. Chicago & London, The University of Chicago Press.

Fisher, J.M. (ed.) 1986: *Moral Responsibility.* 1986. Ithaca & London, Cornell University Press.

Fisher, J M. and M. Ravizza (eds.) 1993: *Perspectives on Moral Responsibility.* 1993. Ithaca & London, Cornell University Press.

Flam, H. 1992: "Emotional Man: Corporate Actors as Emotion-Motivated Emotion Managers" in Mary Zey (ed.): *Decision Making: Alternatives to Rational Choice Models.* 1992. Sage Publications, pp. 129-139.

Frank, R 1988: *Passions Within Reason.* 1988. New York & London, W.W. Norton.

Frankena, W.K. 1980: *Thinking About Morality.* 1980. Ann Arbor, University of Michigan Press.

Frankfurt, H.G. 1971: "Freedom of will and the concept of a person" *Journal of Philosophy* 1971. No. 1.

Frankfurt, H.G. 1988: *The Importance of What We Care About.* 1988. Cambridge, Cambridge University Press.

Freeman, E.R. 1984: *Strategic Management: A Stakeholder Approach.* 1984. Minneapolis, Pitman.

Frey, B.S. 1997: *Not Just for the Money: An Economic Theory of Personal Motivation.* 1997. Cheltenham, Edward Elgar Publishing.

Fox, W. 1990: *Toward a Transpersonal Ecology.* 1990. Boston, Shambhala.

Gasparski, W. 2002: "Effectiveness, Efficiency, and Ethicality in Business and Management" in L. Zsolnai and W. Gasparski (eds.): *Ethics and the Future of Capitalism.* 2002. New Brunswick and London, Transaction Publishers, pp. 117-136.

Gilligan, C. 1982: *In a Different Voice: Psychological Theory and Women's Development.* 1993. Cambridge and London. Harvard University Press.

Goodpaster, K.E. and J.B. Matthews 1982: "Can a Corporation Have Conscience?" *Harvard Business Review* 1982. No 1. pp. 132-141.
Goodpaster, K.E. 1983: "The Concept of Corporate Responsibility" *Journal of Business Ethics 19&3.* Nol.pp. 1-22.
Goodpaster, K.E. 1991: "Business Ethics and Stakeholder Analyses" *Business Ethics-Quarterly* 1991. No. 1.
Granovetter, M. 1985: "Economic Action and Social Structure: The Problem of Embeddedness" in Mary Zey (ed.): *Decision Making: Alternatives to Rational Choice Models.* 1992. Sage, pp. 304-333.
Hardin, G. 1968: "The Tragedy of the Commons" *Science* 1968 December, pp. 1243-1248.
Harsanyi, J.C. 1975: "Can the Maximin Principle Serve as a Basis for Morality? A Critique of John Rawls' Theory" *The American Political Science Review* 1975. pp. 594-606.
Hart, H.L.A. 1961: *The Concept of Law.* 1961. Oxford, Oxford University Press.
Hartman, N. 1966: *Teleologisches Denken.* 1966. Berlin, Walter de Gryter.
Hausman, D. M. and M.S. McPherson 1996: *Economic Analyses and Moral Philosophy.* 1996. Cambridge, Cambridge University Press.
Heidegger, M. 1977: *The Question Concerning Technology and Other Essays.* 1977. New York, Harper & Row.
Herrnstein, R.J. 1961: "Relative and absolute strength of response as a function of frequency reinforcement" *Journal of Experimental Analyses of Behavior.* 1961. pp. 267-272.
Herrnstein, R.J. 1970: "On the law of effect" *Journal of Experimental Analyses of Behavior* 1970. pp. 243-266.
Herrnstaein, R.J. 1993: "Behavior, Reinforcement, and Utility" in Michael Hechter, Lynn Nadel & Richard E. Michod (eds.): *The Origin of Values.* 1993. New York, Aldine de Gruyter. pp. 137-152.
Hirschleifer, J. 1994: "The Dark Side of the Force" *Economic Inquiry,* 1994 January.pp. 1-10. Hoffman, M.W. 1984: "The Ford Pinto" in W. Michael Hoffman & Robert E. Frederick (eds.): *Business Ethics.* 1995. McGraw-Hill, Inc. pp. 446-454.
Holmes, S. 1990: "The Secret History of Self-Interest" in Jane J. Mansbridge (ed.): *Beyond Self-Interest.* 1990. Chicago & London, The University of Chicago Press. pp. 267-286.
Jacobs, M. 1996: "Environmental Valuation, Deliberative Democracy and Public Decision-Making Institutions." Paper presented for the *Inaugural Conference of European Society for Ecological Economics.* May 1996. Universite de Versailles St Quentin en Yvelines, France.
Jencks, C. 1990: "Varieties of Altruism" in Jane J. Mansbridge (ed.): *Beyond Self-Interest.* 1990. Chicago & London, The University of Chicago Press, pp. 53-67.
Jonas, H. 1966: *The Phenomenon of Life: Toward a Philosophical Biology.* 1966. Harper & Row, New York. Jonas, H. 1974: *Philosophical Essays: From Ancient Creed to Technological Man.* 1974. Englewood Cliffs, NJ, Prentice-Hall. Jonas, H. 1979: *Das Prinzip Verantwortung. Versuch einer Ethic fur die Technologische Zivilization.* 1979. Frankfurt am Main, Insel Verlag.
Jonas, H. 1984: *The Imperative of Responsibility: In Search of an Ethics for the Technological Age.* 1984. Chicago & London, The University of Chicago Press.
Jonas, H. 1994: "Philosophy at the End of the Century: A Survey of its Past and Future" *Social Research* 1994. No 4. pp. 812-832.

Kahneman, D. 1994: "New Challenges to the Rationality Assumption" *Journal of Institutional and Theoretical Economics* 1994. No. 1. pp. 18-36.

Kahneman, D. andA. Tversky 1979: "Prospect Theory: AnAnalysis of Decision Under Risk" *Econometrica* 1979 March, pp. 263-291.

Keeney, R.L. and H. Raiffa 1976: *Decisions with Multiple Objectives: Preferences and Value Tradeoffs.* 1976. New York, Wiley.

Kirschenmann, P.P. 1991: "Moral and Other Responsibilities of Science and Technology" in Creighton Peden & Yeager Hudson (eds.): *Communitarianism, Liberalism, and Social Responsibility.* 1991. Lewiston/Queenston/Lampeter, The Edwin Mellen Press, pp. 89-109.

Leopold, A. 1948: *A Sand County Almanac.* 1984. Oxford, Oxford University Press.

Levi, I. 1986: *Hard Choices.* 1986. Cambridge, Cambridge University Press. Lichtenstein, S. and P. Slovic 1971: "Reversal of Preference Between Bids and Choices in Gambling Decisions" *Journal of Experimental Psychology.* 1971 January, pp. 46-55.

Lovelock, J. 1979: *Gaia. A New Look at Life on Earth.* 1979. Oxford, Oxford University Press.

Lucas, J.R. 1995: *Responsibility.* 1995. Oxford, Clarendon Press.

MacCrimmon, K.E. and D.M. Messick 1976: "A Framework for Social Motives" *Behavioral Science* 1976. No. 1.

MacCrimmon, K.E. 1995: "A Radical Proposal—Relating Decision Theory to Real Decisions: Current Gaps as Future Research Opportunities" in *Decision under Uncertainty.* 1995. Sienna, University of Sienna. C.N.R. pp. 265-301.

Maclntyre, A. 1981: *After Virtue.* 1981. Notre Dame, University of Norte Dame Press.

Maclntyre, A. 1988: *Whose Justice? Which Rationality?* 1988. Notre Dame, University of Norte Dame Press.

Main, M., N. Kaplan and J. Cassidy 1985: "Security in infancy, childhood, and adulthood: A move to the level of representation" in I. Bretherton & E. Walters (eds.): *Growing Points of Attachment Theory and Research.* 1985. Monographs of the Society for Research in Child Development, pp. 66-106.

Mansbridge, J.J. 1990: "On the Relation of Altruism and Self-Interest" in Jane Mansbridge (ed.): *Beyond Self-Interest.* 1990. Chicago & London, The University of Chicago Press, pp. 133-143.

Mansbridge, J.J. (ed.) 1990: *Beyond Self-Interest.* 1990. Chicago & London, The University of Chicago Press. Margulis, L. 1998: *Symbiotic Planet. A New Look at Evolution.* 1998. New York, Basic Books.

Maturana, H. and F. Varella 1980: *Autopoiesis and Cognition.* 1980. Dordrecht, Holland, D. Reidel. McDaniel, C.N. & J. Gowdy 2000: *Paradise for Sale. A Parable of Nature.* 2000. Berkeley, Los Angeles, London, University of California Press.

Meadows, D. et al. 1972: *The Limits to Growth.* 1972. Cambridge, MIT Press.

Mitroff, I. 1998: *Smart Thinking for Crazy Times. The Art of Solving the Right Problems.* 1998. San Francisco, Berrett-Koehler Publishers, Inc.

Naess, A. 1989: *Ecology, Community and Lifestyle.* 1989. Cambridge, Cambridge University Press.

Nagel, T. 1986: *The View from Nowhere.* 1986. New York. Oxford University Press. Nagel,T. 1988: "Autonomy andDeontology"rnSamuelScheffler(ed.):Con,se<jrwenft'a/z',s»2 *and its Critics.* 1988. Oxford, Oxford University Press, pp. 142-172.

Nozick, R. 1974: *Anarchy, State, and Utopia.* 1974. New York, Basic Books.

O'Neill, O. 1992: "Duty and Obligation" in Lawrence C. Becker & Charlotte B. Becker (eds.): *Encyclopaedia of Ethics.* 1992. New York & London, Garland Publishing, Inc. pp. 273-278.

Passerin d'Entreve, M. 1992: "Communitarianism" in Lawrence C. Becker & Charlotte B. Becker (eds.): *Encyclopaedia of Ethics.* 1992. New York & London, Garland Publishing, Inc. pp. 181-185.

Pearce, D. 1993: *Economic Value and the Natural World. 1993. London,* Earthscan Publications.

Pincoffs, E.L. 1992: "Virtues" in Lawrence C. Becker & Charlotte B. Becker (eds.): *Encyclopaedia of Ethics.* 1992. New York & London, Garland Publishing, Inc. pp. 1283-1288.

Polanyi, K. 1946: *The Great Transformation: Origins of our Time.* 1946. London, Victor Gollancz Ltd.

Post, K.E. 1986: "The ethics of marketing: Nestle's infant formula" in W. M. Hoffman & R. E. Frederick (Eds.): *Business Ethics. Readings and Cases in Corporate Morality.* 1986. New York, McGraw-Hill, Inc. pp. 416-421.

Putman, R.J. and S.D. Wraten 1984: *Principles of Ecology.* 1984. Los Angeles, University of California Press.

Rawls, J. 1971: *A Theory of Justice.* 1971. Cambridge, Harvard University Press.

Saaty,T.L. 1980: *The Analytic Hierarchy Process.* 1980. New York, McGraw-Hill. Inc.

Sandel, M. 1982: *Liberalism and the Limits of Justice.* 1982. Cambridge, Cambridge University Press.

Scheffler, S. 1988: "Introduction" in S. Scheffler (ed.): *Consequen-tialism and its Critics.* 1988. Oxford, Oxford University Press, pp. 1-13.

Schumacher, E.F. 1973: *Small is Beautiful: Economics as if People Mattered.* 1973. London, Abacus.

Selten, R. 1994: "New Challenges to the Rationality Assumptions" *Journal of Institutional and Theoretical Economics* 1994. No. 1. pp. 42-44.

Sen, A. 1970: "The Impossibility of a Paretean Liberal" *Journal of Political Economy* 1970. pp.152-157.

Sen, A. 1977: "Rational Fools: A Critique of the Behavioural Foundations of Economic *Theory" Philosophy and Public Affairs* 1977. pp. 317-344.

Sen, A. 1982: "Rights and Agency" in S. Scheffler (ed.): *Consequentialism and its Critics.* 1988. Oxford, Oxford University Press, pp. 187-223.

Sen, A. 1983: "Evaluator Relativity and Cosequentialist Evaluation" *Philosophy and Public Affairs* 1983. pp. 113-132.

Sen, A. 1985: "Rights as Goals" (Austin Lecture 1984) in S. Guest & A. Milne (eds.): *Equality and Discrimination: Essays in Freedom and Justice.* 1985. Stuttgart, Franz Steiner. pp. 11-25.

Sen, A. 1987: *On Ethics and Economics.* 1987. Oxford, Blackwell. Sen, A. 1992: "Minimal liberty" *Econometrica* 1992. pp. 139-159.

Sen, A. 1992: *Inequality Reexamined.* 1992. New York & Oxford, Russel Sage Foundation and Clarendon Press.

Sen, A. and B. Williams (eds.) 1982: *Utilitarianism and Beyond.* 1982. Cambridge, Cambridge University Press.

Simon, H.A. 1976: *Administrative Behavior.* 1976. New York, The Free Press.

Simon, H.A. 1977: "The Structure of 111-Structured Problems" in H. A. Simon: *Models of Discovery and Other Topics in the Methods of Science. 1911.* Dordrecth, Holland, D. Reidel Publishing Company, pp. 304-325.

Simon, H.A. 1978: "Rationality as Process and as Product of Thought" *American Economic Review* 1978 No. 2. pp. 1-16.

Simon, H.A. 1982: *Models of Bounded Rationality.* 1982. Cambridge & London, The MIT Press.

Simon, H.A. 1987: "Satisficing" in *The New Palgrave: A Dictionary of Economics.* 1987. London, Macmillan. pp. 243-245.

Simon, H.A. et al. 1992: "Decision Making and Problem Solving" in Mary Zey (ed.): *Decision Making: Alternatives to Rational Choice Models.* 1992 Sage Publications. pp. 32-53.

Slote, M. 1992: "Consequentialism" in Lawrence C. Becker & Charlotte B. Becker (eds.): *Encyclopaedia of Ethics.* 1992. New York & London, Garland Publishing, Inc. pp. 211-214.

Soros, G. 1998: *The Crisis of Global Capitalism.* 1988. London, Little, Brown and Company.

Stewart, T.J. 1992: "A Critical Survey on the Status of Multiple Criteria Decision Making Theory and Practice" *OMEGA (International Journal of Management Science)* 1992. Nos. 5-6. pp. 569-586.

Shweder, R.A. 1986: "Divergent Rationalities" in R.W. Fiske & R.A. Shweder (eds.): *Metatheory in the Social Sciences: Pluralism and Subjectivities.* 1986. Chicago, The University of Chicago Press.

Taylor, C. 1985: *Philosophical Papers.* 1985. Cambridge, Cambridge University Press.

Thaler, R.H. 1991: *Quasi Rational Economics.* 1991. New York, Russell Sage Foundation.

Tversky, A. and D. Kahneman 1981: "The Framing of Decisions and the Psychology of Choice" *Science* 1981 January 31. pp. 453-458.

Tversky, A. and D. Kahneman 1986: "Rational Choice and the Framing of Decisions" *Journal of Business* 1986 No 4. pp. 251-278.

Tversky, A. and D. Kahneman 1991: "Loss Aversion in Riskless Choice: A Reference-Dependent Model" *Quarterly Journal of Economics* 1991. pp. 1039-1061.

Tversky, A. and D. Kahneman 1992: "Advances in Prospect Theory: Cumulative Representation of Uncertainty" *Journal of Risk and Uncertainty* 1992. pp. 297-323.

Ullman-Margalit, E. 1977: *The Emergence of Norms. 1911.* Oxford, Clarendon Press.

van Uzendoorn, M.H. and H.A. Zwart-Woudstra 1995: "Adolescents' Attachment Representations and Moral Reasoning" *The Journal of Genetic Psychology* 1995. No. 3. pp. 359-372.

von Neumann, J. and O. Morgenstern 1944: *Theory of Games and Economic Behavior.* 1944. Princeton, Princeton University Press.

von Weizsacker, C.F. 1971: *Die Einheit der Natur.* 1971. Miinchen, Carl Hauser Verlag. von Winterfeldt, D. and W. Edwards, 1986: *Decision Analysis and Behavioral Research.* 1986. Cambridge, Cambridge University Press.

Walzer, M. 1983: *The Spheres of Justice.* 1983. New York, Basic Books.

Weber, M. 1921-1922: *Economy and Society.* 1968. New York, Bedminster Press.

Williams, B.A. 1988: "Reinforcement, Choice, and Response Strength" in R.C. Atkinson et al. (eds.): *Stevens'Handbook of Experimental Psychology.* 1988. New York, Wiley. Volume 2. pp. 167-244.

Wolf, S. 1982: "Moral *Saints" Journal of Philosophy* 1982. pp. 419-439.

Zamagni, S. (ed.) 1995: *Economics of Altruism.* 1995. Chettelham, Allen Edgar.

Zapffe, P.W. 1996: *On the Tragic* (in Norwegian). 1996. Oslo, Pax Forlag AS.

Zeleny, M. 1995: "Trade-Offs—Free Management" *Human Systems Management* 1995 No. 3.

Zimmerman, M.J. 1988: *An Essay on Moral Responsibility.* 1988. Totowa, N.J

Zimmerman, M.J. 1992: "Responsibility" in Lawence C. Becker & Charlotte B. Becker (eds.): *Encyclopaedia of Ethics.* 1992. New York & London, Garland Publishing, Inc. pp. 1089-1095.

Zsolnai, L. 1991: "Morally Rational Decisions" in Attila Chikan (ed.): *Progress in Decision, Utility and Risk Theory.* 1991. Kluwer Academic Publishers, pp. 293-298.

Zsolnai, L. 1993: "Responsible Choice in Complex Socio-Economic Situations." Paper presented for the *Second International Conference on Public Service Ethics.* June 1993, University of Sienna, Italy.

Zsolnai, L. 1995: "I, We, and She: An Ecological Note on Etzioni's I & We Paradigm" *The Journal of Socio-Economics* 1995. No. 3. pp. 521-524. Zsolnai, L. 1996: "Environmental Ethics for Business" *Management Research News* 1996. No. 10. pp. 9-15.

Zsolnai, L. 1996: "Moral Responsibility and Economic Choice" *InternationalJournal of Social Economics* 1997. No. 4.

Zsolnai, L. (ed.) 2002: *Ethics in the Economy: Handbook of Business Ethics.* 2002. Oxford & Bern, Peter Lang Academic Publishers.

Zsolnai, L. and K.J. Ims (eds.) 2006: *Business within Limits: Deep Ecology and Buddhist Economics.* 2006. Oxford, Peter Lang Academic Publishers.

Index

About the Author

Laszlo Zsolnai is professor and director of the Business Ethics Center at the Corvinus University of Budapest. He is chairman of the Business Ethics Inter-faculty Group of the Community of European Management Schools (CEMS). He is editor-in-chief of the Interdisciplinary Yearbook of Business Ethics at Peter Lang Academic Publisher in Oxford.

Laszlo Zsolnai was born in 1958, in Szentes, Hungary. He has a master's in finance and a doctorate in sociology from the Budapest University of Economic Sciences. He received his PhD and DSc degrees in economics from the Hungarian Academy of Sciences. He was teaching and researching at University of California at Berkeley, Georgetown University, University of Oxford, Norwegian School of Economics and Business Administration, Helsinki School of Economics, Bocconi University Milan, EHSAL Brussels, Vienna University of Economics, Europe-University of Viadrina, Central European University, Royal Netherlands Academy of Sciences, University of Antwerp, Venice International University, London School of Economics, University of Edinburgh, University College London, European University Institute (Florence) and the International Institute for Applied Systems Analyses (IIASA).

Laszlo Zsolnai is editorial board member of the *International Journal of Social Economics, International Journal of Spirituality and Management, Business Ethics: An European Review, Finance and the Common Good, Society and Economy,* and *Society and Business Review, International Journal of Green Economics* and *Journal of Human Values.*

Laszlo Zsolnai's books include the following:

- *The European Difference.* 1998. Kluwer Academic Publishers, Boston-Dordrecht-London.
- *Ethics and the Future of Capitalism.* 2002. Transactions Publisher. New Jersey-London (with Wojciech Gasparski).
- *Ethics in the Economy: Handbook of Business Ethics.* 2002. Oxford and Bern: Peter Lang Academic Publisher.
- *Spirituality, Ethics and Management.* 2004. Kluwer Academic Publishers, Boston-Dordrecht-London.
- *Business Within Limits: Deep Ecology and Buddhist Economics.* 2005. Oxford and Bern: Peter Lang Academic Publisher (with Knut Johannessen Ims).
- *Spirituality as a Public Good.* 2007. Garant. Antwerp, (with Luk Bouckaert).